SPIRITUALITY FOR SALE

i

SPIRITUALITY FOR SALE

BABAJI

To seekers who dare to walk past the circus to the truth beyond.

Spirituality for Sale

Contents

PROLOGUE

Harper handed over his car keys, his wedding ring, and the deed to his house because the spiritual teacher explained that his "attachment to material possessions" was blocking his ascension to higher consciousness. Three months later, he was sleeping in his sister's garage while his former guru posted Instagram stories from his new beachfront mansion.

Welcome to the spiritual circus.

The big tent stretches before you, all flashing lights and impossible promises. Step right up! Enlightenment in just one weekend! Ancient wisdom, now with easy payment plans! The ringmaster's smile gleams as he counts your money, and the performers know exactly which tricks make seekers like you reach for their wallets.

You wandered in here because something's missing. Life feels flat despite all your achievements. You sense reality runs deeper than what you've been told. Maybe you're just tired of feeling lost in your own existence.

The circus performers have been watching people like you for years. They know your weak spots better than you do.

This book is your guide to spotting their tricks before you become part of the show.

The compound guru builds his empire one devoted follower at a time, creating a spiritual kingdom where he's the only one who really "gets it." The weekend warrior packages thousand-year-old wisdom into digestible workshops, stripping out everything that made it actually work. The digital shaman accumulates Instagram followers while his real life crumbles behind the perfectly filtered posts.

Then there are the fortune tellers—unlicensed therapists who've learned that "intuitive counseling" pays better than actual credentials. They'll read your energy field for $200 an hour, but somehow always discover you need a marriage spell, career spell, or spiritual cleansing. Pet readings included, because even your dog apparently needs psychic intervention.

The psychedelic evangelists promise shortcuts to states that traditionally took monks decades to reach. Just one ceremony and you'll understand the universe! Never mind that you still can't handle a difficult conversation with your mother.

The gift shop sparkles with solutions: crystals that will shift your vibration, supplements that will open your third eye, courses that guarantee awakening if you just follow their simple system. Each purchase feeds the illusion that consciousness can be upgraded like a smartphone.

Here's what they don't tell you: real spiritual development is about as glamorous as learning to play piano. It requires daily practice, honest self-examination, and the kind of patience that doesn't photograph well for social media.

The stakes go deeper than your bank account. Bad spiritual teachers can shatter your ability to trust your own judgment. Premature exposure to advanced practices can destabilize psychological structures that took years to build. Spiritual bypassing becomes a sophisticated way to avoid dealing with ordinary human responsibilities—using mystical concepts to escape rather than engage with reality.

But you have something the circus performers fear: the capacity to think for yourself.

You can learn to spot the teacher who demands absolute loyalty while tolerating zero questions. You can recognize the community that slowly isolates you from friends and family who might offer reality checks. You can identify practices designed to create dependency rather than independence.

The real masters exist—they're just not performing under the big tent. They don't need flashy websites or promises of instant transformation. They're out there doing quiet work, often completely unknown to the spiritual marketplace.

But first, you need to navigate the circus without losing your shirt, your sanity, or your ability to recognize sound guidance when you finally encounter it.

The performers have learned to speak the language of your deepest longings. They promise relief from suffering, meaning in confusion, power in helplessness. They wear robes of borrowed wisdom and speak in voices honey-sweet with manufactured compassion.

You're about to learn their game inside and out.

By the time the final curtain falls, you'll spot spiritual con artists from three tents away. You'll know which red flags to watch for, which promises are too good to be true, and which practices are designed to keep you coming back for more rather than setting you free.

The circus is in full swing. The lights are flashing, the music is playing, and the crowd is mesmerized by promises they desperately want to believe.

Welcome to the carnival of modern-day spirituality. The show is about to begin.

Ego: The Endless Search

Welcome to the main tent. You've stepped past the ticket booth, and now the real show begins. The lights are brighter here, the promises louder, and your wallet suddenly feels heavier in your pocket. That's not an accident.

Remember Harper? He's not the only one. Meet Sienna, who dropped $3,200 on a "soul activation intensive" that left her more confused than when she started. Or Omar, who spent $800 on "chakra realignment" with a "master healer" who learned his trade from YouTube videos. The stories pile up like carnival tickets— each one representing someone who came seeking truth and left with an empty bank account and a head full of spiritual jargon.

The moment you start asking life's big questions, the circus operators light up like slot machines. They've been studying people like you for years, mapping your weak spots with the precision of a military campaign.

The Business of Seeking

Want instant awakening? Lucky you—there's a retreat for that, only $4,500 plus airfare to Costa Rica. Need your chakras aligned? That'll be $200 with a "Certified 4th degree Reiki Healer" who got her certificate from a series of weekend workshops. Craving connection with your spirit guides or a lost loved one? Online mediums now offer introductory rates as low as $1 per minute!

These aren't fringe operators working from dingy storefronts. This is big business. The global wellness industry pulls in over

$4.4 trillion annually, and spiritual services are its fastest-growing segment. Your seeking mind isn't just a customer—you're a demographic, carefully studied and precisely targeted.

The operators know exactly what buttons to push. Feeling disconnected? They'll sell you community. Lacking purpose? They've got your life mission mapped in the stars. Struggling with relationships? Your 75 minute twin flame psychic romance reading is just a $244.44 fee away. They've weaponized your deepest longings and turned them into marketing copy.

Here's their playbook: Take ancient practices that once required decades of discipline, strip away the hard parts, add mystical language, and package it for people who want transformation without effort. Meditation becomes "mindfulness apps." Yoga becomes "spiritual fitness." Prayer becomes "manifestation coaching."

It's spiritual fast food—tastes great going down, gives you a temporary high, but leaves you hungrier than before. And just like fast food, it's designed to be addictive. The moment one technique stops working, they've got three more waiting in the wings.

What's Really Running the Show

Before we go deeper into the circus, you need to understand what brought you here in the first place. It wasn't just curiosity or life circumstances—it was something more fundamental running the show behind the scenes.

That voice in your head that never stops commenting? The one that says "I need this" and "I don't like that" and "Why did this happen to me?" That's not actually you—that's your ego. And it's the circus operators' favorite customer.

Think of the ego as your internal narrator—the voice that's constantly commenting on your experience, claiming ownership of everything: "My job, my problems, my spiritual journey, my enlightenment." It's the part that whispers "I am this body, these thoughts, these roles, these achievements."

It builds its identity from borrowed materials: your name, your memories, your social roles, your wins and losses. It decorates this construction with beliefs—some inherited, some acquired—and defends it as if it's the only home you'll ever have.

Here's the thing—the ego started as a useful function. It helps you differentiate your body from the world around you, forms preferences, protects your individual existence. But somewhere along the way, this helpful assistant staged a coup. The servant crowned itself king and convinced you it was running the whole kingdom.

Picture a wave convinced it's separate from the ocean and struggling to maintain its individual form. Or an actor so lost in character they defend the costume as if their life depends on it. The ego experiences itself as isolated, constantly seeking to fill a void that exists only in its imagination.

The Ego's New Costume

Now here's where spiritual seeking gets tricky. When you start questioning everything, the ego doesn't panic—it adapts. It trades its business suit for robes, swaps wine for kombucha, and suddenly it's "the spiritual one."

This is crucial to understand because the ego doesn't disappear when you start seeking truth—it just gets a spiritual makeover. The ego loves this upgrade. It gets to feel special, evolved, further along than all those unconscious people still trapped in materialism. It secretly craves recognition—even for how humble it appears. Especially for how humble it appears.

Watch this in action: The person who can't stop talking about the latest addition to their crystal collection. The newly enlightened friend who suddenly speaks only in spiritual platitudes. The retreat veteran who name-drops their latest teachers like trophies. Same narrator, different script.

The ego-as-seeker becomes the circus's most reliable customer. It mistakes every unfamiliar spiritual experience for awakening, every new practice for progress, every teacher's validation for truth. The same mind that leads you into confusion offers to guide you out—for a price.

The Illusion Machine

The circus operators understand something most seekers don't: you're not actually looking for more experiences. You're looking to stop the endless searching. You want the restless mind to finally be quiet. You want to feel whole instead of constantly reaching for the next thing to fill the void.

But "inner peace through not buying anything" doesn't make for good marketing copy.

So they flip the script. Instead of helping you see through the illusion of separation, they sell you better separation. Premium separation. Artisanal, small-batch, organic separation with a no refund policy.

They point you everywhere except where you need to look: inward. "Go there." "Do that." "Follow this teacher." "Sign up for that retreat." "Try this sacred plant medicine." The promise is always just one purchase away—somewhere out there.

It's like rowing a boat that's still tied to the dock. You sweat, you strain, you might even feel like you're making progress. But you're still in the same place, mistaking motion for movement.

The Real Target Market

The circus doesn't want enlightened customers—enlightened people stop buying spiritual products. They want seekers: people who feel close to breakthrough but never quite get there. People who get just enough relief to keep coming back but never enough resolution to stop searching.

Think about it: if these approaches actually delivered permanent transformation, wouldn't the businesses go bankrupt? If weekend "soul-healing" retreats actually brought lasting peace, wouldn't people stop attending them? If meditation apps actually delivered transformation, wouldn't people cancel their subscriptions?

The business model depends on your continued dissatisfaction. They need you hungry but not fed, hopeful but not fulfilled, always one purchase away from the breakthrough that somehow never comes.

Your Spiritual Compass

Here's your first navigation tool: Ask yourself whether what you're considering makes you more dependent or more independent. Real spiritual development increases your ability to handle life's challenges without external support. Spiritual entertainment creates dependency on the provider.

Does the teacher point beyond themselves toward your own capacity, or do they position themselves as indispensable? Does the practice increase your ability to be present with ordinary life, or does it require increasingly exotic experiences to maintain its effect?

Most importantly: Are you reaching for truth, or just a more comfortable illusion?

That question is your compass. No guru, no app, no technique can answer it for you. It's the one thing the circus can't sell you—your own capacity for honest self-examination.

The Path Forward

You're standing at the edge of this circus because something real stirred inside you. That stirring was legitimate. The hunger for meaning, for truth, for an end to the endless searching—that's the most natural thing in the world.

But what you're seeking isn't in the tents, the apps, or the next big retreat. It's not hidden in ancient secrets or exotic locations. It's closer than your next breath, more immediate than this moment, as available as the awareness that's reading these words right now.

The circus is designed to keep you looking everywhere except where the answer actually is. It's strategically positioned between your initial curiosity and your eventual recognition of what you truly are—like a massive gift shop placed between the parking lot and the temple.

This chapter was your orientation. Now you know what you're walking into and why it's designed the way it is. The rest of this book will be your field guide—not to give you answers, but to help you spot the traps, navigate the distractions, and remember what you're actually seeking when the barkers try to convince you it's for sale.

The show is about to get more elaborate. But now you know you're watching a performance, not participating in your own transformation.

Keep your eyes open and your wallet closed. The real journey is just beginning.

2

The Gift Shop of Spirituality

Before the path deepens, most seekers pass through the gift shop. It's not always a literal store—it's the stage in your journey where objects, rituals, and "energetic tools" seem like the key to unlocking truth. Crystals promise abundance, tarot cards offer guidance, sage bundles pledge purification. They feel sacred, mysterious, and just within reach of your credit limit.

The truth? They're the appetizers of the spiritual feast— designed to whet your appetite for transformation while keeping you perpetually hungry. And the people serving them? Many genuinely believe in what they're offering, which makes them less obviously dangerous than clear con-artists, but no less capable of leading you astray when you stop to ask for directions.

In the shadowy corners of these establishments sit the theatrical fortune tellers—those crystal ball gazers whose cold reading techniques are so transparent they barely warrant discussion. "I see change coming," they intone, as if change weren't the one constant in human existence. These carnival barkers deal in Barnum effect platitudes, generic enough to fit anyone desperate enough to pay for validation.

Far more seductive are the gift shop's subtler offerings: the citrine pyramids that supposedly magnetize wealth, the oracle decks that claim to channel divine wisdom, the white sage bundles that promise to cleanse your energetic field. These occupy the treacherous middle ground between ancient wisdom and modern wishful thinking.

Watch how it works: The crystal vendor arranges her specimens with museum-quality reverence, each stone supposedly calibrated to specific frequencies that will unlock your dormant potential. Rose quartz for love, amethyst for awakening, citrine for abundance. The scientific mind knows these are mineral formations created by geological pressure over millennia—but the seeking heart wants to believe that Earth's ancient processes might hold keys to personal transformation.

The tarot reader shuffles her deck with ceremonial precision, each card supposedly containing archetypal wisdom that illuminates your path forward. The rational observer recognizes pattern recognition and psychological projection—the mind's compulsion to find meaning in randomness. Yet even skeptics pause when a spread seems to speak directly to their secret struggles.

These practices exist in the fertile borderland between psychology and spirituality, between legitimate self-reflection tools and expensive placebos. Some contain genuine value—the ritual of card drawing can prompt introspection, the weight of a beautiful stone can anchor wandering attention, the ceremony of burning herbs can mark transitions between mental states.

But the marketplace promises far more than these modest benefits. It promises transformation, healing, answers to existence's deepest riddles—all available for immediate purchase, no patience required.

The real tragedy isn't that people seek meaning through objects and rituals—humans have always used physical symbols to connect with the sacred. The tragedy is how the gift shop corrupts this impulse, transforming meaningful spiritual hunger into consumer behavior. Instead of pointing toward the patient inner work that genuine transformation requires, these offerings suggest that enlightenment can be bought, wisdom can be acquired, awakening can be achieved through the right combination of crystals, cards, and ceremonies.

The seeker arrives hungry for truth and leaves with a shopping bag full of spiritual accessories, each one carrying the promise that this will be the tool that finally works. But tools can't do the work for you—they can only distract you from the recognition that what you're seeking was never missing in the first place.

Consider Eli, who stood at the threshold of just such a shop, convinced that somewhere among its glittering promises lay the answer to his unnamed longing. His story illuminates how even the most sincere spiritual hunger can be transformed into something far more ordinary—a consumer's quest for the perfect product to fill an un-fillable void.

What he discovered in that temple of spiritual commerce reveals something crucial about the nature of seeking itself, and why the gift shop stands like a glittering barrier between the seeker's initial awakening and the simple recognition of what they truly are.

⟋⟍

The Gift Shop Pilgrim

Eli paused at the door of the spiritual gift shop, the faint jingle of a bell slicing through the hum of the street outside. The air wafted out, heavy with sandalwood and something sweeter— maybe rosewater, maybe hope. Inside, shelves loomed like altars, stacked with glinting crystals, silk-wrapped tarot decks, and sage bundles tied with twine so perfect they could've been art. His chest tightened, a mix of nerves and longing. This could be it, he thought. The place where I finally find my answers.

At 28, Eli was adrift in a life that felt like a half-finished sketch —job decent but uninspiring, friends drifting into marriages and mortgages, a vague ache he couldn't name. He'd sampled the usual fixes: therapy, self-help books, a gym stint that lasted but a few weeks. Nothing stuck. But this shop, with its aura of something greater, beckoned like a flare in the fog of his ordinary existence.

The modern seeker's dilemma crystallizes in moments like these—standing at the threshold between the mundane and the mystical, hungry for transformation but uncertain of the path. The gift shop offers itself as a bridge between worlds, its wares promising to translate ancient wisdom into contemporary convenience. It's spiritual fast food for souls starving on a diet of material success and emotional emptiness.

From behind a curtain of beads, the shopkeeper appeared, her smile radiant, her eyes alight with a knowing glow. Her shawl flowed like liquid dusk, and her presence carried the scent of mystery made manifest. "Greetings, seeker," she purred, her voice a soothing balm for nerves he didn't know were frayed. "Are you ready to step into your higher vibration?"

Eli's sneakers squeaked as he shifted, feeling suddenly conscious of his ordinary clothes in this temple of the extraordinary. "I'm... looking for something. Not sure what. Something to make me feel... more like me."

What do I even mean when I say "me"? He quietly thought to himself as he stood there awkwardly gawking at this exotically dressed shopkeeper. The question hung in his mind like incense smoke—persistent, intangible, impossible to grasp but somehow essential.

She tilted her head, appraising him with the practiced eye of someone who'd seen countless variations of the same spiritual hunger. "A sacred quest," she declared, her tone imbuing his confusion with cosmic significance. "The items here can illuminate your path. What's missing, dear one?"

He hesitated, feeling exposed under her knowing gaze. "Purpose, I think. Connection." *Connection to what, though?* He quickly thought to himself, realizing he was using words without understanding their weight. "I have this curiosity... but no answers and no direction."

Her smile widened, a spark of certainty in her gaze that felt both reassuring and somehow predatory. "Then let's awaken your journey and pave the path ahead of you."

As she led him deeper into the shop, past displays of amethyst clusters and Buddha statues mass-produced in distant factories, Eli caught sight of a small alcove tucked behind a beaded curtain. A hand-painted sign announced "Psychic Readings - Divine Guidance - $50." The booth itself was a masterpiece of theatrical spirituality: purple velvet draped over a folding card table, a crystal ball that caught the shop's dim lighting like trapped starlight, and

13

sitting behind it all, a woman whose age seemed to shift with the shadows, her dark hair threaded with silver, her fingers heavy with rings that caught light like captured promises.

"Madame Esperanza," the shopkeeper whispered, following Eli's gaze. "She sees what others cannot. Very gifted. Very accurate."

Something in Eli's chest fluttered—not quite hope, not quite fear, but something between them. The rational part of his mind, the part that balanced checkbooks and met deadlines, whispered warnings about charlatans and cold reading. But the part that had brought him here, the part that ached for something more than the daily grind, leaned forward with hungry curiosity.

"Maybe after we explore some tools for your journey," the shopkeeper suggested, her tone carefully casual. "Madame Esperanza works better with those who've already begun awakening their spiritual senses."

The sales strategy was subtle but effective—create hierarchy, suggest readiness, imply that spiritual tools were prerequisites for higher mysteries. Eli found himself nodding, allowing her to guide him toward the citrine pyramid that gleamed first, its golden edges dancing in the shop's soft light.

***

Eli reached for the citrine pyramid, tentative, and the shopkeeper glided over with practiced grace. "Citrine," she exclaimed, pressing it into his hand with ceremony that transformed the simple exchange into ritual. "A radiant key to abundance. It aligns your solar plexus, drawing wealth and dissolving energetic stagnation. A true gift from the universe."

The weight of the crystal in his palm felt simultaneously grounding and thrilling. *Abundance.* The word unfurled in his mind like a flower, carrying with it images of his debts shrinking, his stress easing, his life finally clicking into the harmony he'd always felt was just out of reach. "How's it work?" he asked, his voice carrying a mix of skepticism and desperate hope.

14

"Intention," she whispered, leaning close enough that he could smell the patchouli oil in her hair. "Place it where your spirit rests —your bed, your workspace. Speak your truth to it. The energy answers those who call with pure hearts."

The explanation was beautifully vague, scientifically meaningless, and emotionally perfect. It placed the responsibility for results squarely on Eli's shoulders while positioning the crystal as an infallible conduit for cosmic forces. If it worked, the crystal deserved credit. If it didn't, his intention wasn't pure enough, his heart wasn't open, his spirit wasn't aligned.

"How much?" His wallet was already out, pulled by an urgency he couldn't quite explain.

"Thirty-five," she said with the tone of someone offering a precious gift at a fraction of its true value. "A modest exchange for prosperity's embrace."

At home, he perched the citrine pyramid on his desk, nudging aside a pile of ignored mail that suddenly seemed like evidence of his spiritual poverty. *Here we go,* he thought, feeling both foolish and hopeful. *Money, peace, a life that actually makes sense.* That night, he murmured to the crystal: "Bring me what I need." The words stumbled out, awkward and unfamiliar on his tongue, but he pressed on, picturing paychecks stacking up, opportunities flowing like water toward his newfound spiritual magnetism.

Days ticked by with the relentless precision of ordinary time. A week passed. His email remained stubbornly devoid of life-changing offers, his bank balance as static as ever. *Patience,* he told himself, eyeing the pyramid that seemed to mock him with its unchanging golden gleam. Maybe it was misplaced. He shifted it to his nightstand, then back to his desk. He scoured the internet late into the night— "citrine charging," "crystal activation," "abundance manifestation"—soaking the stone in moonlight, rinsing it in salt, speaking to it with increasingly desperate affirmations.

Still, no shift. Doubt slithered into his consciousness like smoke under a door. *Am I doing it wrong? Am I not enough?* The questions multiplied, each one carrying a payload of shame that settled in his chest like sediment. He buried the thoughts, clutching the shopkeeper's promise. *Intention. Trust the process. It'll come.*

But a stone can't attract prosperity. Your attention can. The citrine pyramid, for all its crystalline perfection, is nothing more than organized silicon dioxide—beautiful, ancient, but as financially inert as the dust on his windowsill. The real magic lies in the attention paid, the intention set, the mental focus directed toward abundance. But it's easier to believe in the stone—it asks nothing from you except belief, and belief feels like progress when you're lost in the wilderness of your own unfulfilled life.

The tragedy isn't that the stone doesn't work. The tragedy is that the stone becomes a substitute for the inner work that actually does. Instead of examining his relationship with money, his patterns around scarcity, his deeper beliefs about worthiness, Eli focuses on the external tool, hoping for transformation without the discomfort of genuine change.

After two weeks of citrine disappointment, Eli found himself drawn again to the gift shop, seeking either validation or an upgrade to his spiritual arsenal. This time, Madame Esperanza's booth called to him like a siren song. The purple velvet seemed deeper in the afternoon light, the crystal ball more luminous, the psychic herself more mysterious behind her curtain of silver-streaked hair.

"Sit, dear one," she intoned before he'd even approached, her voice carrying the gravitas of someone who'd witnessed cosmic secrets. "I've been expecting you."

The opening gambit was perfect—unexpected enough to suggest genuine psychic ability, vague enough to apply to anyone who'd been circling the shop with obvious uncertainty. Eli felt a thrill of recognition, as if the universe itself had orchestrated this moment.

He settled into the folding chair across from her makeshift altar, noting how the booth's arrangement seemed to focus all attention on her weathered face, shadowed just enough to seem mysterious, lit just enough to read his expressions. "I've been... seeking," he began hesitantly.

"Of course you have," she replied with knowing warmth. "I see it in your aura—brilliant gold, but fragmented. You've been hurt recently. Something to do with your work life, yes? Or perhaps a relationship that didn't unfold as expected?"

Eli's breath caught. The description felt eerily accurate—his job dissatisfaction, his recent breakup with Hana, the general sense of being scattered across too many unfulfilling pursuits. He nodded slowly, leaning forward despite himself.

Madame Esperanza wasn't psychic. She was observant. The slight tension in his shoulders spoke of work stress. The way he'd glanced at couples walking past the shop suggested romantic disappointment. His presence in a spiritual gift shop on a weekday afternoon indicated someone seeking answers, likely someone whose conventional life wasn't delivering satisfaction. The "brilliant but fragmented aura" description could apply to virtually anyone—most people see themselves as having unrealized potential scattered across life's demands.

"I see a journey ahead," she continued, her fingers dancing above the crystal ball as if reading invisible currents. "Travel, perhaps. Or maybe an inner journey—a spiritual awakening that will reshape everything. There's a teacher coming into your life. Someone wise, older perhaps, who will guide you toward your true calling."

The predictions were masterfully crafted—broad enough to encompass numerous possibilities, positive enough to generate hope, specific enough to feel personally meaningful. Travel could be anything from a vacation to a new job to a metaphorical journey of self-discovery. The wise teacher could be anyone from a therapist to a yoga instructor to a character in a book that provided insight.

"But beware," she added, her voice dropping to a theatrical whisper, "there are obstacles. I see deception around you. Someone close to you doesn't want you to grow, doesn't want you to find your power. They may seem supportive, but their energy is... clouded."

Now Eli was fully hooked. The warning felt both ominous and empowering—he was important enough to have enemies, special enough to threaten others with his potential growth. His mind immediately began scanning his relationships for signs of sabotage, reinterpreting normal interactions through the lens of spiritual warfare.

"Your parents," Madame Esperanza continued, reading the subtle shift in his posture as he considered the "deception" warning. "I sense their energy around this blockage. Love, but also... limitation. They want to keep you small, keep you safe, keep you from flying too high."

The insight felt profound, deeply personal, almost uncomfortably accurate. Of course his parents wanted to keep him safe—all parents did. Their natural concern for his stability could easily be reframed as spiritual limitation, their practical advice recast as energetic sabotage. This wasn't psychic ability; this was psychology wrapped in mystical language, universal family dynamics presented as cosmic revelation.

"What should I do?" Eli asked, his voice smaller than he'd intended.

"Trust yourself," she replied, gesturing toward the crystal ball as if it held his reflection rather than distorted light. "The answers are within you, but they've been clouded by others' fears. I can help clear that energy, help you connect with your higher guidance. For a small additional offering, I can perform a cleansing ritual, remove the psychic blocks that are keeping you from your destiny."

The upsell was smooth as silk—reframe his uncertainty as external interference, position herself as the solution, create urgency around his spiritual development. For another fifty dollars, she could burn some sage, light a candle, speak some phrases in what might have been Latin or might have been theatrical nonsense, and send him away feeling temporarily empowered.

But something in Eli's chest contracted. Maybe it was the way her eyes briefly flicked to his wallet when he hesitated. Maybe it was the awareness that he'd just spent thirty-five dollars on a rock that had failed to transform his life. Maybe it was a small, quiet voice that whispered: *If the answers are within me, why am I paying someone else to find them?*

"I... I need to think about it," he said, standing on unsteady legs.

Madame Esperanza's smile didn't waver, but something cooled in her eyes. "Of course, dear one. But don't wait too long. The energies I've seen tonight are time-sensitive. Your window for this particular awakening won't stay open forever."

The final manipulation—scarcity, urgency, fear of missing out. But Eli was already backing away from the booth, suddenly seeing the cardboard edges beneath the velvet draping, the LED lights behind the crystal ball, the ordinary woman playing an extraordinary role.

He mumbled his thanks and retreated toward the shop's main floor, feeling both disappointed and oddly relieved. The psychic reading had given him exactly what he'd craved—validation, importance, cosmic significance—but it had also shown him something else: his own desperate hunger for external validation, his willingness to hand over authority for his own life to anyone who spoke with confidence about his destiny.

***

The tarot deck called next, its box painted with a starry wanderer Eli couldn't place—a figure suspended between earth and sky, carrying symbols that seemed to whisper of hidden meanings and secret knowledge. He lingered before the display, and the shopkeeper swooped in with practiced timing, her shawl grazing him like moth wings.

"The Rider-Waite," she announced with reverence, cradling the deck as if it were a sacred relic. "Your intuition is strong—I can sense it. This deck is a bridge to your soul's wisdom. It unveils your destiny, aligning you with cosmic truth."

The flattery hit its mark. After the mixed experience with Madame Esperanza, the suggestion that his own intuition might be the key felt both validating and empowering. Here was a tool that wouldn't require him to trust anyone else's interpretations—just his own inner knowing working through ancient symbols.

"What does it tell me?" Eli asked, his voice thin with hope barely concealed.

"Everything," she replied with the confidence of someone who'd never doubted the cards' infallibility. "Your purpose, your heart, your next move. Shuffle with clarity, draw with faith. The cards speak truth to those who listen with open souls."

He shelled out twenty-five dollars and raced home with the urgency of someone who'd finally found the missing piece of life's puzzle. On his living room rug, legs crossed in what he imagined was a spiritually appropriate posture, he shuffled the cards with reverent concentration. The glossy surfaces slipped through his fingers like whispered promises, each one carrying the weight of potential revelation.

What's my way forward? he asked silently, then drew three cards with the solemnity of prayer. They fell face-up before him: The Tower—a lightning-struck spire crumbling into chaos; The

Fool—a figure stepping playfully toward a cliff's edge; The Wheel of Fortune—an enormous wheel spinning with cryptic symbols.

The guidebook's pages blurred under his eager gaze as he searched for meaning. Disruption, new beginnings, cycles of change. The interpretations felt simultaneously profound and frustratingly vague, like poetry that touched something deep without ever quite revealing what that something was.

The next day, he drew again: The Lovers, The Moon, Death. Choice, illusion, transformation. The cards seemed to spin elaborate stories in the air above his coffee table, tales of romance and deception, ending and renewal. But the stories kept shifting, elusive as smoke, mocking his attempts to pin them down into actionable guidance.

Each morning became a ritual of seeking, the cards his daily oracle, his compass through the wilderness of an ordinary life that suddenly felt charged with mystical significance. But the more he drew, the more he realized the cards were mirrors, reflecting his own hopes and fears back at him in symbolic form. The meanings he found were the meanings he brought to them, dressed in the language of cosmic inevitability.

Am I blind to their message? he wondered after a particularly frustrating session where five different spreads had yielded five different visions of his future. *Do I need lessons? Another deck? A proper teacher?* The shop's "no refunds" policy stung like salt in a wound he'd inflicted on himself, and he finally slid the deck aside with the bitter taste of disappointment coating his tongue.

***

Eli craves a compass, but tarot spins a kaleidoscope. His ego's lost, spinning for meaning, while the self sits whole, laughing gently at the mind's endless need to complicate what simply is. The irony is almost too perfect—his mind's chasing a path that Eli is already walking. Have you ever hunted desperately for what's been waiting patiently in your stillness? Vague guidance feels profound when you're desperate for direction. When you want answers badly enough, even random images become prophecy, coincidence transforms into destiny, and confusion masquerades as mystery.

The cards themselves aren't evil or useless. They're neutral symbols that can serve as prompts for introspection, mirrors for self-reflection, catalysts for conversations with the unconscious mind. In the hands of someone grounded in genuine self-awareness, they can be valuable tools for psychological exploration. But in the hands of the desperate seeker, they become another external authority, another way to avoid the patient work of developing inner discernment.

***

The sage bundle caught Eli's eye last, its earthy scent tugging at something primal in his awareness as he lingered by the counter, defeated by crystals and cards but not yet ready to surrender his quest. The dried herbs were bound with twine the color of sandstone, their gray-green leaves whispering promises of purification and renewal.

"Your place feeling a bit heavy lately?" the shopkeeper asked with uncanny timing, lifting the sage bundle like a beacon of hope. "This white sage is like a reset button for your energy field. Light it, walk it through your rooms, and it'll clear out all the psychic funk. You'll feel lighter, I promise."

The language was perfect—clinical enough to sound legitimate ("psychic funk"), mystical enough to feel sacred ("energy field"), practical enough to seem achievable ("reset button"). After weeks of metaphysical disappointment, the sage offered something tangible, a ritual he could perform with his own hands rather than relying on stones or cards to work their mysterious magic.

"Does it actually work?" Eli pressed, his skepticism belligerent with desperate hope.

"Oh, absolutely," she said, her eyes bright with conviction that felt genuine. "Indigenous peoples have been using sage for thousands of years to clear negative energy from sacred spaces. I personally sage my place every single day—it's like spiritual hygiene."

The appeal to ancient authority was masterful—connecting the practice to indigenous tradition while conveniently omitting the cultural context, ceremonial protocols, and spiritual frameworks that gave such rituals their original meaning and power. Sage became a spiritual disinfectant, divorced from the prayer, intention, and community that once surrounded its sacred use.

That night, Eli sparked the bundle with the solemnity of someone performing surgery on his own soul. The flame hissed alive, then settled into a steady smolder that filled his apartment with smoke so thick it triggered his fire alarm. He fanned the bundle frantically, sending pungent clouds swirling through his small rooms like incense in a temple designed by someone who'd never actually been in a temple.

Clear it out, he commanded fiercely, his eyes watering from the smoke as he swept the smoldering sage through doorways and around furniture. He imagined his accumulated disappointments dissolving, his romantic failures evaporating, his career dissatisfaction burning away like morning fog. The bundle smoldered and sparked, demanding constant attention to maintain its glow, and he stood in the haze waiting to feel some profound shift in his apartment's invisible atmosphere.

The smoke gradually dissipated through opened windows, carrying with it his hopes for instant purification. The weight of his unchanged life remained, settling back into his consciousness like dust after a brief windstorm. *Focus harder,* he muttered to himself, already planning his return to the shop for palo santo, frankincense, and whatever other sacred aromatics might succeed where white sage had failed.

His place began to smell like a New Age temple, layers of sacred smoke building into an aromatic archaeology of spiritual seeking. Myrrh, Sandalwood, Dragon's Blood—each new scent carrying fresh promises of energetic cleansing, each one leaving him feeling more spiritually accomplished and less actually transformed. The apartment became a museum of olfactory enlightenment, but his mind remained as restless as ever, churning through the same patterns of dissatisfaction dressed in increasingly exotic fragrances.

Eli's burning sage to chase away shadows, but his mind's the one casting them. The smoke can't clear the thoughts that keep him awake at night, can't purify the emotional patterns that repeat like broken records, can't cleanse the spiritual hunger that drives him to seek quick fixes for problems that require patient inner work. Ritual without inner stillness is just scented performance, ceremony divorced from the consciousness that gives it meaning.

The irony cuts deep: ancient sages and yogis did indeed burn incense, their smoke curling through temples and meditation caves, calming the air and setting the stage for deep practice. But they understood that the external ritual was meant to support internal discipline, that the sage cleared the space for the real work of sitting with themselves, facing their minds, dissolving the ego's endless demands for entertainment and validation.

Eli's mind clings to the smoke itself, as if the right combination of sacred scents could burn away the spiritual confusion it creates with every desperate grasp for external transformation. The weight isn't in his apartment's energy field—it's in the seeking mind that refuses to rest long enough to discover what's already whole, already clear, already present beneath the smog of spiritual materialism.

Eli slumped in his favorite chair, surrounded by the failed treasures of his spiritual quest: the citrine pyramid collecting dust on his windowsill like a golden paperweight, the tarot deck scattered across his coffee table in arrangements that spelled nothing but confusion, sage ash dusting his apartment like the remains of burned hopes. He palmed the crystal one more time, feeling its cool weight against his skin.

Just a rock, he thought with the clarity that sometimes emerges from complete disillusionment. The insight wasn't bitter—it was liberating. The cards were paper, beautifully illustrated but ultimately empty of the cosmic significance he'd projected onto them. The sage was dried plant matter, aromatic and ancient in its own right, but powerless to cleanse anything beyond the staleness of closed windows and stagnant air.

He could've kept chasing, of course. The gift shop offered endless variations on the theme of external salvation: cacao ceremonies promising to "open his heart," twin flame readings to help him "find his soul's mirror," Akashic records sessions to "unlock past-life keys to present-day blocks." All sparks of promise, all glimmers of possibility, but none the fire he truly craved—the steady flame of genuine understanding burning within his own awareness.

The shopkeeper's enthusiasm echoed in his memory, and he recognized now that her belief was completely real. She genuinely trusted in the citrine's abundance-drawing properties, sincerely believed in the cards' prophetic powers, authentically experienced the sage as energetically purifying. But belief, however sincere, isn't truth. Conviction, however passionate, doesn't create reality. The fact that she believed didn't make the beliefs accurate—it just made her a true believer rather than a conscious charlatan.

Why did I buy into it? he wondered, examining his own psychology with the detached curiosity of a scientist studying specimens. The answer emerged in layers: his hunger for meaning in a life that felt spiritually empty, his need for guidance in a world that offered endless choices but little wisdom, his desire for transformation without the patience required for genuine inner work.

The ancient traditions from which these practices originated understood something crucial that the gift shop had forgotten: the external tools were meant to support internal discipline, not replace it. Sacred smoke did curl through temples and ashrams, but it served practitioners who spent years learning to quiet their minds, to face their shadows, to surrender the ego's endless demands for comfort and validation.

Maybe the incense helped steady their concentration for meditation. Maybe the crystals served as focal points for attention during long hours of contemplation. Maybe the symbolic systems like tarot provided frameworks for psychological exploration when wielded by those who'd already developed deep self-awareness.

But Eli's mind had clung to the smoke itself, hoping the right combination of spiritual accessories could burn away the restlessness they were meant to calm. The weight wasn't out there in his apartment's energy field or encoded in crystal matrices or hidden in card spreads—it was in the seeking mind that refused to be still long enough to discover what was already present, already whole, already perfect beneath the fog of spiritual consumerism.

He stepped outside into the night air, sharp and clean after hours of sage smoke. A plain stone in his yard caught his eye—gray, unremarkable, shaped by wind and rain rather than human intention. He held it in his palm, feeling its simple weight, its honest coolness, its complete lack of marketing claims or mystical promises. No glow emanated from its surface, no cosmic energy pulsed through its ordinary matter. It was just being itself—fully, completely, without pretense or performance.

A whisper rose from somewhere deeper than thought: *What if it's not about adding anything? What if it's about letting go?*

Eli held that ordinary stone from his yard, feeling its honest weight against his palm. No cosmic energy pulsed through its gray surface. No abundance flowed from its crystalline structure. It simply existed—complete, un-marketed, making no promises it couldn't keep.

The gift shop's true nature crystallized in that moment. Not a gateway to enlightenment, but a marketplace where spiritual hunger gets transformed into consumer appetite. The citrine pyramid on his windowsill caught the morning light, beautiful and inert. The scattered tarot cards spelled nothing but his own projections. The sage ash dusting his furniture marked rituals that had cleared nothing but his bank account.

These weren't malicious deceptions. The shopkeeper's enthusiasm was genuine, Madame Esperanza's mystical performance heartfelt. They believed in their offerings as sincerely as Eli had wanted to believe in them. But belief, however passionate, doesn't create the reality it claims to reveal.

The marketplace works precisely because it promises the impossible: transformation without effort, wisdom without patience, awakening without the uncomfortable work of facing yourself. It takes the human impulse toward the sacred—ancient, legitimate, necessary—and repackages it as spiritual fast food. Quick, convenient, ultimately unsatisfying.

Eli's apartment still smelled faintly of sandalwood and disappointment. The fire alarm had been triggered not by spiritual purification but by too much dried plant matter burning in too small a space. The abundance he'd whispered to his crystal pyramid remained as elusive as ever. The cards had offered him a dozen different futures, none more accurate than educated guessing dressed in mystical language.

The real invitation had been quieter than the shop's glittering displays: stop seeking long enough to notice what was never missing. The awareness reading these words existed before his first spiritual purchase and would remain after his last. It needed no enhancement, no alignment, no activation through ancient minerals or sacred ceremonies.

This recognition didn't make him cynical about authentic spiritual practice. It made him discriminating. The difference became clear: genuine discipline involves the patient work of training attention and dissolving the ego's grip on experience. Spiritual materialism feeds the very patterns that wisdom traditions were designed to transcend.

The consciousness that seeks through crystals and cards must ultimately turn inward, beyond all objects, to discover its own nature. No external tool can do the work that only awareness itself can accomplish—the simple recognition of what it already is.

But recognizing the gift shop as spiritual theater doesn't end the seeking. It only graduates the seeker to more sophisticated performances. When crystals and tarot cards fail to deliver promised transformation, the hunger for transcendence intensifies. The next tent beckons with far more dramatic promises—not just abundant living or cosmic guidance, but complete ego dissolution, union with the divine, and direct access to ultimate reality itself.

The stage grows larger, the promises more intoxicating, the potential for both genuine insight and catastrophic delusion exponentially greater. After all, if gentle sage smoke and crystal meditation couldn't crack open the doors of perception, perhaps it's time for something that promises to blow them off their hinges entirely.

3

The Psychedelic Detour

When crystals fail to deliver abundance and tarot cards refuse to reveal destiny, the seeker's hunger sharpens into something more desperate. The gift shop promised transformation through objects, but objects remain stubbornly inert. The ego, frustrated by these gentle failures, begins scanning for more dramatic solutions. If meditation apps and sage bundles can't crack open the doors of perception, perhaps it's time for something that promises to dissolve the doors completely.

Enter the psychedelic renaissance—substances that don't merely hint at mystical experience but deliver it with pharmaceutical precision. Unlike the gift shop's vague promises, these compounds offer something measurably real: altered consciousness, ego dissolution, direct encounters with what feels like ultimate reality itself.

The science backing these claims is legitimate. Johns Hopkins researchers have documented psilocybin's capacity to reset depression in ways that outlast traditional pharmaceuticals. Their studies show 75% of participants with major depression feeling significantly better after just two guided sessions, with 58% maintaining that improvement a year later. MDMA demonstrates similar effectiveness for trauma, creating windows where the brain can rewire fear patterns that have persisted for decades.

This isn't pseudoscience or wishful thinking. Brain scans reveal measurable changes: the default mode network—responsible for self-referential thinking and ego maintenance—temporarily dissolves under psychedelic influence. The rigid neural pathways that lock people into repetitive thought patterns suddenly become fluid, allowing new connections to form. For those suffering from treatment-resistant depression, PTSD, or addiction, these substances offer hope where conventional medicine has failed.

But here's where legitimate medicine intersects with the spiritual marketplace in ways that would make any circus operator envious. The same ego that sought salvation through crystals now encounters substances that can temporarily dissolve its boundaries entirely. The experience feels more real than anything the gift shop could deliver—and it is. The visions are vivid, the emotional catharsis profound, the sense of cosmic connection undeniably visceral.

Ayahuasca ceremonies promise direct access to plant consciousness and ancestral wisdom. Psilocybin retreats offer "mystical experiences" with the gravitas of scientific backing. LSD micro-dosing communities speak of enhanced creativity and spiritual insight. These aren't carnival fortune tellers making vague predictions—these are compounds with measurable neurological effects, often administered in settings that blend clinical precision with spiritual ceremony.

The seeker who once wondered if their citrine pyramid was properly charged now finds themselves dissolving into pure consciousness, experiencing states that feel more fundamentally true than ordinary reality. The contrast is overwhelming. Where crystals whispered, psychedelics roar. Where tarot cards hinted, these substances reveal with documentary clarity.

Yet something crucial gets lost in the translation from therapeutic context to spiritual seeking. The controlled clinical settings that produce those impressive statistics—trained therapists, careful screening, months of integration work—bear little resemblance to the consciousness-tourism industry that has grown up around these substances.

The spiritual marketplace has discovered something irresistible: substances that actually deliver genuine altered states. The ego experiences genuine dissolution. The sense of cosmic unity isn't imagination—it's measurable neurological change.

But temporary transcendence isn't permanent transformation, and this gap becomes the next frontier for spiritual commerce. Retreat centers promise "life-changing journeys" for thousands of dollars. Underground facilitators offer "sacred plant medicine" with the authority of ancient tradition. Integration coaches specialize in helping you "embody your insights" through ongoing sessions and workshops.

The seeker enters this realm no longer wanting trinkets—they want direct experience of the divine. And psychedelics, unlike previous spiritual tools, can deliver that experience. The question becomes: what happens when the chemistry wears off and ordinary consciousness returns?

Consider Zara, standing before a tent that promises not symbolic insight but direct revelation—not metaphors for transformation but the real thing, brewed from plants that have guided consciousness for millennia. Unlike previous seekers browsing possibilities, she faces something that will unquestionably alter her perception of reality. The only question is whether that alteration will serve her awakening or feed more sophisticated spiritual seeking.

The Veil of Visions

Zara wandered the carnival's winding paths, drawn by currents she couldn't name. The night air carried whispers—distant laughter, the rustle of fabric, voices promising revelations just beyond hearing. Crystal stalls caught streetlight and threw it back fractured. Tarot readers bent over cards in pools of candlelight, their murmurs weaving through the darkness.

Something felt different here, though she couldn't place what. The shadows seemed deeper, more attentive. Time moved with a strange weight, each step forward feeling significant in ways her rational mind dismissed but her body recognized. She found herself listening for something—a call, a sign, an invitation she'd know when it arrived.

Then—there.

A tent that breathed.

Its canvas walls expanded and contracted with organic rhythm, fabric sighing like sleeping flesh. The structure existed in its own pocket of space where physics bent gracefully around intention.

Light seeped through the weave not from bulbs or flames but from something older, as if the tent itself had learned to glow through centuries of holding sacred darkness.

The Veil of Visions read the sign, letters shifting color with each heartbeat—indigo to violet to black so deep it curved back toward luminescence.

Before her hand reached the entrance, the fabric parted like water.

What emerged wasn't quite human—presence more than form, her midnight robes flowing like liquid shadow that had learned to hold shape. She moved with the certainty of tide and mountain, existing at the edge of perception where sight becomes knowing. Her being carried scents that had no earthly source: the sweetness of rain on dry earth from storms that fell upward, smoke from fires that burned cold, the metallic tang of time itself oxidizing.

"You've been circling," her voice arrived from multiple directions, as if the tent itself spoke through her throat.

Zara blinked, reality reassembling around the words. "I was just —"

"Seeking what seeks you." The being's eyes held depths that moved—not the surface of pupils but spaces between stars. "Enter."

Enter. The word reverberated through dimensions of meaning, each echo carrying different invitations, different warnings.

Inside, the tent unfolded into impossibilities. What should have been a small space stretched toward horizons that curved back on themselves. The air tasted alive, thick with crushed leaves that released their dreams when breathed, metallic undertones that sang of transformation in frequencies her bones could hear.

Cushions arranged themselves in geometries that pleased some mathematical sense she didn't know she possessed. At the circle's heart, a low table materialized—not appeared, but *became*—bearing cups that steamed with liquid darkness.

The being poured with fluid grace, liquid darkness flowing from vessel to cup in a single continuous motion. The cup settled into Zara's palms, warm and substantial, carrying weight beyond its physical form.

"This opens what was never closed," the being intoned, words rippling through layers of reality. "How far depends on how much you can remember to forget."

Zara lifted the cup. The liquid moved like living shadow, tasting of earth's first rain, iron from stars being born, bitterness that clung like ancient sorrow reluctant to release its grip. She swallowed, feeling it spiral down not just her throat but through dimensions of herself she'd never suspected.

The tent's geometry shifted—walls becoming more walls, shadows growing shadows of their own. Colors deepened past their names into territories where blue touched eternity and red whispered secrets in languages older than speech. The carpet beneath her dissolved into waves that carried the memory of every footstep ever taken upon its surface.

Her eyes closed without permission.

Falling.

But falling upward through layers of light that had been disguised as darkness, each stratum revealing itself as crystalline awareness pretending to be space. Visions bloomed like time-lapse flowers: meadows where every blade of grass sang its own note in a symphony that was her heartbeat expanded across geological time. A river of molten meaning flowed with currents that carried not water but pure understanding, each drop a lifetime of accumulated wisdom returning to its source.

Then—the voice. Not heard but absorbed through every cell: *You are not separate.*

The words dissolved the last boundaries. She *was* the meadow, the river, the light that painted shadows so shadows could know themselves as temporary theater. Love expanded through her chest like a nova, erasing every edge, every story, every small self that had ever believed in its own isolation.

This is it, she recognized with cellular certainty. *I am home.*

But in that recognition—the faintest tremor. Mind, ancient in its cunning, slipping through the opened door like mist through cracks. *Remember this,* it urged with seductive urgency. *Hold it. Share it. You are the one who has seen.*

Images cascaded unbidden: herself speaking to crowds hung on every enlightened word, guiding others with the authority of someone who had touched the infinite and returned. The ego, master shapeshifter, already weaving new stories from the very fabric of egoless experience.

In the grasping—distortion. The river's gold tarnished to brass. The meadow's song warped into discord. Debris surfaced in the flowing understanding: masks she'd worn, performances she'd

34

given, the thousand ways she'd hidden from herself floating like corpse-flowers in poisoned water.

A coldness began—not temperature but the absence of what had been flowing through her. The love that had filled every cell drained away through some hairline crack in her being, leaving behind a vacuum that pulled at her essence with inexorable gravity.

Fear didn't arrive—it *unveiled* itself as what had always been there, patient beneath every joy, waiting behind every moment of connection. Not emotion but environment, not feeling but the very atmosphere of a dimension where light had never learned to exist.

The visions collapsed into themselves. Meadow became wasteland. River became cracked earth stretching toward horizons that promised only more emptiness. Her body, moments before dissolved into cosmic consciousness, now felt impossibly dense— lead bones in a mercury world, anchored to some weight that pulled her away from everything that mattered.

She existed in the space between living and dying, where breath continued but brought no air, where awareness persisted but illuminated only absence. Each second stretched into geological eras of experiencing nothing, of being trapped in the gap between heartbeats with no promise that the next would ever come.

This wasn't death—death would have been mercy. This was *un-being*, existence stripped of its capacity to exist, consciousness aware of its own emptiness like an eye forced to see its own blindness. Time became unmeasured suspension in the place furthest from light, where even darkness was too substantial, too present.

Somewhere beyond layers of void, the voice whispered again— distant as forgotten prayer: *The light was never gone. You have turned away.*

But turning required muscles she no longer possessed, volition that had dissolved in the acid of absolute fear.

Eternity.

Moment.

The taste of earth and iron returned to her mouth like messages from a world she'd half-remembered. Weight settled back into her bones, but gently now, like dust remembering how to be dust. When her eyes opened—*when?*—the tent had returned to tent-ness, though its walls still breathed with subtler rhythms.

The being sat beside her, now more woman-shaped but still carrying infinities in her edges. "You met yourself," she offered, extending water that tasted of mountain springs and mercy. "All of yourself."

Zara drank, each drop returning her to form. "It felt like I lost everything," she whispered, voice emerging from depths she hadn't known existed.

The being's gaze held steady as stone, soft as candlelight. "Nothing was lost. You are what you were seeking to keep."

Outside, carnival sounds drifted through fabric walls—laughter that remembered how to be joy, music that had made peace with rhythm, voices calling to each other across distances that could be crossed. Zara stepped back into night air that felt kind against her skin, carrying something indefinable—not enlightenment, not

36

answers, but the strange gift of having descended as far as consciousness could fall and discovered she could still emerge.

The tent behind her continued its patient breathing, holding space for the next seeker ready to meet themselves in dimensions they'd never suspected existed.

Zara stumbled out of that tent carrying something the gift shop could never deliver: genuine altered consciousness. The dissolution of boundaries had been real, the cosmic love undeniable, the vision of interconnection as vivid as any experience in her ordinary life. No crystal or card reading could compete with what she'd encountered in those depths of expanded awareness.

But notice what happened in that space between revelation and grasping. The moment her ego registered the profundity of the experience, it immediately began cataloging, claiming, strategizing. The very mind that had temporarily dissolved started rebuilding itself around the experience, already imagining her as someone special—the teacher, the guide, the one who had touched something ultimate.

The crash that followed wasn't the substance leaving her system. It was the return of her usual psychological patterns, now starkly visible against the backdrop of what she'd glimpsed. The fear, the emptiness, the sense of separation—these weren't created by the brew. They were always there, temporarily dissolved but not permanently resolved. The medicine had simply lifted the curtain on what ordinary consciousness usually keeps hidden.

This is where psychedelics reveal their double edge. Unlike the gift shop's false promises, these compounds deliver authentic mystical experience. The brain scans don't lie—consciousness genuinely expands, ego boundaries truly dissolve, profound insights actually emerge. But the experience unfolds within the same psychological structure that seeks it. The ego that hungers for transcendence is the same ego that tries to possess it once it arrives.

Zara touched something real in that tent, something that couldn't be purchased or performed. But the touching was temporary, and temporary touching isn't permanent transformation. The vision dissolves, ordinary consciousness returns, and the seeker finds themselves in a peculiar position: they've glimpsed the mountain's peak but still stand at its base, now acutely aware of both the summit's reality and their distance from it.

The ache that follows genuine psychedelic experience cuts deeper than any frustration with inert crystals. This isn't disappointment with false promises—it's the recognition that something ultimate exists but seems to slip through every attempt to grasp it. The memory becomes both treasure and torment, proof that expanded consciousness is possible but apparently beyond ordinary reach.

Here's where the spiritual marketplace reveals its most sophisticated trap. Having delivered genuine mystical experience, it now offers to help you keep it. Integration coaches promise to help you "embody your insights." Retreat centers offer progressive journeys deeper into the mystery. Teachers emerge who claim to live permanently in the state you've only visited temporarily.

The seeker who once bought crystals hoping for abundance now faces a more complex hunger: they've tasted what feels like ultimate reality and discovered it can't be held. The question transforms from "What can help me feel better?" to "Who can teach me to sustain what I've touched?"

The substances themselves become less important than the search for someone who can bridge the gap between experience and embodiment. The ego, having failed to possess transcendence directly, now seeks to possess it indirectly through the right teacher, the perfect method, the ultimate practice that will make permanent what chemistry made temporary.

This drives seekers toward the circus's most dangerous performances—not the obvious charlatans but the sophisticated teachers who promise what no substance can deliver: awakening on demand. The hunger sharpened by real transcendent experience becomes the very force that propels them toward those who claim to hold the keys to permanent transformation.

The ultimate irony runs deeper than any substance can reach: what Zara touched in that moment of dissolution—the recognition of what she truly is—never actually departed. The light didn't disappear when the chemistry changed; her attention simply turned away from it. But recognizing this requires a different kind of work than any substance can perform, a patient returning to what was glimpsed rather than a desperate seeking of what seems lost.

Yet few are willing to sit with this possibility when teachers appear who promise to restore what was never actually missing. The path curves away from underground ceremonies and retreat centers toward spiritual teachers who claim to embody permanently what the substances revealed temporarily. The very legitimacy of the mystical experience becomes the credential that validates the teacher's authority—and the seeker's conviction that someone, somewhere, must know how to make the temporary permanent.

The Lost Guide

In the modern spiritual marketplace, anyone can become a teacher by Tuesday. A single weekend of instruction. A laminated certificate. A fresh profile picture posed before a Himalayan tapestry. And suddenly, the mantle of "guide," "healer," or "guru" is acquired with varying degrees of self-awareness.

This isn't to say every newly certified instructor is a charlatan. Many are sincere, even well-meaning. But sincerity and depth are not the same thing. The current wellness and spirituality industries have carved a fast track for those hungry to teach—one that often bypasses the years of disciplined practice, self-inquiry, and humble apprenticeship that once formed the backbone of spiritual leadership.

This hunger to teach doesn't appear from nowhere. It's often born in the young seeker whose world has just split open. Maybe they've touched altered states through psychedelics or stumbled into mystical insight through meditation. Perhaps they've experienced profound healing from trauma, a moment of ego dissolution, or a glimpse of what mystics call "unity consciousness." Suddenly, the veil between "normal" and "something more" has thinned, and they can't unsee what they've seen.

Their everyday life—the job, the errands, the small talk at parties—feels pale by comparison. Returning to the old rhythms of the 9-to-5 feels like betrayal of the profound truth they've touched. Without a clear path forward, they search for purpose in the only direction that now feels alive: the spiritual path. And in a culture where meaning has been commodified, that path forward is often paved with "become a teacher" programs—an appealing way to not only stay immersed in the new worldview but also make a living within it. The ego, still intact despite the spiritual opening, whispers seductively: You've been chosen. You understand what others don't. You have a gift to share.

But here's what these newly awakened seekers often don't realize: no matter how transformative, a single experience isn't enough to shoulder the responsibility of guiding others. Peak experiences are like lightning strikes—brilliant, transformative, but momentary. The real work of spiritual development happens not in the flash of insight but in the slow, often unglamorous process of integration. It's one thing to glimpse the mountain; it's quite another to learn every path up its face, to understand where each trail leads and where each becomes treacherous.

The Assembly Line of Instant Expertise

In this culture, credentials have become spiritual currency, and the market has responded accordingly. Short, intensive programs offer the allure of mastery in weeks or even days. You can earn the title of "teacher" after a 200-hour yoga training, which, compressed into consecutive days, amounts to less than a month of study. Life coaching courses are packaged into four-to-eight-week programs, complete with scripts for difficult conversations and branded mantras for social media.

The breath-work training programs have perhaps perfected this model. A few intensive weekends teach participants to facilitate sessions that can catapult others into non-ordinary states of consciousness, complete with emotional catharsis, past-life visions, and mystical revelations. The newly certified facilitator walks away with a toolkit for inducing powerful experiences but often lacks the depth to hold space when those experiences turn challenging or traumatic. They've learned the technique but not necessarily the wisdom to navigate what the technique unleashes.

Consider what breath-work can trigger: the dissolution of psychological defenses built over decades, the surfacing of suppressed memories, intense physical sensations that can mimic heart attacks or panic disorders. A skilled facilitator needs to recognize when someone is having a spiritual breakthrough versus a psychological break, when to encourage deeper surrender and when to help someone ground back into ordinary reality. These distinctions can't be learned from a manual—they require years of personal practice, mentorship, and witnessing hundreds of sessions under experienced guidance.

Yet certification programs regularly graduate facilitators who've observed perhaps a dozen sessions and practiced the techniques on themselves a handful of times. They enter the field equipped with breathing patterns and essential oil recommendations but without the experiential wisdom to recognize when someone's shaking represents therapeutic release versus re-traumatization.

Advanced practice certifications follow similar patterns, compressing traditional apprenticeships that once spanned decades into intensive trainings measured in days or weeks. Students learn techniques and terminology—but without the depth of personal practice and mentorship that traditionally prepared teachers to safely guide others through powerful transformative processes.

The result is a marketplace flooded with well-intentioned but underprepared teachers whose depth of knowledge may be as shallow as the certificate they frame on their wall. But the carnival's entrepreneurial spirit didn't stop with basic certifications —it evolved toward even more elaborate formats designed to maximize both profit and the appearance of spiritual authority.

The Retreat Mirage

As the carnival's basic offerings became commonplace, enterprising teachers recognized an untapped market: seekers willing to pay premium prices for premium experiences. Why settle for a two-hour workshop in a community center when you could have a transformative weekend at a luxury resort? Thus was born the spiritual retreat industry—a brilliant fusion of ancient wisdom and modern hospitality that promised deeper transformation through deeper comfort.

The formula was seductive: intimate groups capped at twelve participants for "individualized attention." Gourmet vegetarian meals prepared by private chefs. Accommodations at boutique

42

resorts overlooking mountains or coastlines. Morning yoga sessions at sunrise, evening meditations by candlelight. Social bonding experiences that created lasting friendships and, more importantly, lasting loyalty to the teacher. Price points that transformed weekend workshops into investment-level commitments—$2,000, $5,000, even $10,000 for a long weekend of "transformation."

But strip away the Egyptian cotton sheets and farm-to-table cuisine, and a curious truth emerges: none of these luxuries have any relationship to the practices being taught. They are cushions for the ego to rest upon—distractions from the often uncomfortable work of genuine transformation. The marble bathrooms and infinity pools serve not the soul's awakening but the ego's comfort, ensuring participants feel special, chosen, deserving of whatever insights the weekend might provide.

The Comfort Trap

Here lies perhaps the retreat industry's most profound contradiction: seeking enlightenment through material comfort. Ancient traditions understood that spiritual growth often required deliberate discomfort—sleeping on hard ground, eating simple food, confronting the ego's demands for luxury. The modern retreat industry has inverted this entirely, selling the fantasy that awakening can be achieved through thread counts and wine pairings. It's spiritual materialism packaged as its opposite, where the very comfort meant to support the journey becomes the barrier to genuine transformation.

Perhaps most insidiously, luxury retreats have become sophisticated mechanisms for spiritual bypassing—using spiritual practices to avoid dealing with real psychological, emotional, or practical problems. The bubble of luxury and artificial community allows participants to feel temporarily enlightened while their actual lives remain unchanged. Why address your marriage problems, financial stress, or career dissatisfaction when you can spend a weekend feeling cosmic and connected?

The retreat setting actively encourages this avoidance. Surrounded by like-minded seekers in a beautiful environment, removed from the pressures and triggers of daily life, everyone feels more peaceful, more loving, more awakened. But this peace is entirely circumstantial—a product of the environment, not genuine transformation. Participants mistake the temporary absence of their usual stressors for spiritual progress, never learning to find equanimity within the chaos of actual existence.

The Experience Economy

The retreat format has evolved into what might be called "transformation theater"—a carefully orchestrated production designed to create artificial peak experiences that feel profound in the moment but collapse under the weight of ordinary life. Sleep deprivation from early morning practices and late-night "sharing circles" creates a heightened state that participants mistake for spiritual breakthrough. Intense group dynamics, often guided by teachers skilled in emotional manipulation rather than genuine wisdom, manufacture cathartic moments that feel like healing but are merely temporary release.

These manufactured highs serve a crucial business function: they create the retreat addiction cycle. Participants return to their regular lives carrying a profound sense that something extraordinary happened to them, but as the afterglow fades, they find themselves booking the next retreat, chasing that manufactured peak. The retreat industry has essentially created the spiritual equivalent of a casino—environments specifically designed to produce intense experiences that keep customers coming back for more.

Modern retreats have become content farms for social media, turning participants into unpaid marketing agents spreading the mirage further. Those sunrise yoga shots overlooking Tulum treetops? The candlelit meditation circles on pristine beaches? They're not documentation of genuine spiritual practice—they're advertisements for experiences that prioritize aesthetics over authenticity.

Participants, having invested thousands in these experiences, become emotionally invested in portraying them as transformative. Their social media posts create a feedback loop of spiritual FOMO,

44

driving more seekers toward these expensive experiences. The teachers, meanwhile, build their brands not through demonstrated wisdom but through curated imagery of beauty and luxury that has nothing to do with the quality of their teachings.

The Business Model

The retreat industry has weaponized spiritual language to justify its pricing structures and manipulate participants into financial commitments that often stretch far beyond their means. "Investment in your spiritual growth" replaces honest pricing discussions. "Trust the universe to provide" becomes code for taking on credit card debt for luxury experiences. "Abundance mindset" shames those who question whether a weekend workshop should cost more than many people's monthly rent.

Payment plans allow participants to commit to experiences they can't afford, while "early bird" discounts and "last chance" messaging create artificial urgency around what are often regularly offered programs. Once participants have made significant financial commitments, the sunk cost fallacy kicks in—they become psychologically invested in believing the experience was worth the money, regardless of its actual value.

This pricing structure also creates a troubling class hierarchy within spiritual spaces. Those who can afford premium retreats are implicitly positioned as more serious about their spiritual growth than those limited to free meditation groups or affordable workshops. The luxury retreat industry thus transforms spiritual seeking—traditionally accessible to all regardless of material wealth—into another arena where economic privilege masquerades as spiritual advancement.

More troubling still, the retreat format has become a hype-generation machine for otherwise unremarkable teachers. A practitioner who might struggle to fill a community center workshop can suddenly position themselves as a sought-after guru by hosting "intimate retreats in sacred locations." The mystique of limited availability, exotic locales, and premium pricing creates an artificial sense of exclusivity and importance around teachings that may be perfectly ordinary—or worse.

Social proof becomes manufactured through the retreat experience itself. When twelve people have each paid $3,000 to attend a weekend retreat, there's tremendous psychological pressure for everyone—participants and teacher alike—to validate that the experience was profound and transformative. This creates an echo chamber of artificial validation that the teacher can then leverage to attract future participants and justify premium pricing.

The Transformation Illusion

Perhaps most damaging is how the retreat industry actively undermines the very transformation it promises to provide. Real spiritual growth requires integration—the patient, often unglamorous work of applying insights to daily life, building consistent practices, and slowly rewiring habitual patterns. But the retreat model is antithetical to integration. It creates peak experiences in artificial environments that bear no resemblance to participants' actual lives.

Genuine teachers of traditional wisdom understand that sustainable transformation happens gradually, through consistent practice within the context of ordinary life. But gradual, sustained growth doesn't generate the kind of dramatic testimonials and social media content that sells retreats. So the industry has evolved to prioritize intensity over sustainability, peak experiences over steady growth, and weekend breakthroughs over lifelong practice.

Most retreat providers offer little to no support for integration once participants return home. There might be a few follow-up emails or access to an online community, but the business model relies on people believing their transformation happened during the retreat itself, not through the months and years of work that would follow.

None of this is to discourage people from enjoying restorative getaways that combine relaxation with spiritual practices. There's nothing wrong with wanting a beautiful environment, good food, and peaceful community while learning meditation or yoga. The problem arises when seekers approach these experiences expecting permanent transformation, or when retreat providers promise transcendence through luxury. A grounded participant can enjoy

46

the temporary peace and insights such experiences offer while understanding them for what they are—refreshing breaks that might inspire continued practice, not ultimate spiritual solutions. The danger lies not in the retreat format itself, but in the delusion that transformation can be purchased and the illusion that comfort leads to enlightenment.

Dangerous Territories

When regulation is absent and credentials meaningless, this marketplace naturally produces its most insidious variations—retreats that exploit the luxury format and spiritual language to mislead seekers in dangerous and deceptive ways. Two examples illustrate what can go wrong when unqualified teachers gain access to vulnerable seekers through the retreat format.

The Dangerous Path: Premature Awakening

In the retreat marketplace's endless hunt for premium experiences, few words carry more magnetic power than "Kundalini" and "Tantra." These ancient Sanskrit terms have become spiritual marketing gold, transforming ordinary weekend workshops into exotic "awakening experiences" with premium price tags. Retreat organizers drop these buzzwords like breadcrumbs, leading seekers toward expensive intensives promising to "harness your spiritual awareness" and "unlock ancient tantric wisdom."

What modern seekers encounter under these sacred names bears virtually no relationship to their authentic origins. These traditional practices were historically kept secret and required years of preparation under experienced masters because of the documented dangers of premature or unsupervised implementation. Ancient practitioners understood the immense physiological, psychological, and energetic risks involved—severe psychological disruption, uncontrollable energy sensations, personality fragmentation, and in extreme cases, complete psychological breakdown requiring years to stabilize. Most critically, these traditions unanimously agreed that such practices should never be undertaken without a highly skilled master overseeing every stage of the process.

Yet retreat marketplaces now offer hundreds of "Awakening Weekends" led by teachers with weekend certifications. Even more dangerous are practitioners who've learned fragmented techniques without understanding their complete context. Modern teachers often cherry-pick powerful practices—specific breathing patterns, energy visualization techniques—while ignoring the extensive preparatory work and safety protocols that made these practices viable. They unknowingly guide participants into energetic territories using half-understood methods that can create experiences easily mistaken for divine interactions.

At best, these retreats produce intense physical sensations, emotional releases, or altered states that participants mistake for genuine spiritual territory. At worst, they trigger psychological destabilization that can leave individuals unmoored from their own lives. The retreat format provides perfect cover for this recklessness—when participants have paid thousands for intimate experiences in beautiful locations, there's tremendous psychological pressure to interpret any intense experience as spiritually meaningful rather than potentially harmful.

The recommendation regarding these paths is clear: don't pursue them. This isn't spiritual gatekeeping—it's recognizing that certain practices require levels of preparation and expertise that simply aren't available through weekend certifications. You wouldn't go skydiving with an instructor whose only qualification was a weekend course and their own recent jump. The same logic applies to practices that can fundamentally alter consciousness and psychological stability. Traditional lineages exist precisely because this work requires deep preparation, constant supervision, and decades of experience to guide safely.

The Ego's Disguise: Sacred Language for Adult Recreation

A different kind of retreat deception exploits spiritual language to rebrand adult sexual experiences as transcendent practices. "Sacred Sexuality" and "Divine Intimacy" retreats promise to help participants "channel sexual energy to higher levels of being" and "increase spiritual connection with the Divine" through what amount to genital massage workshops with Sanskrit names.

48

These retreats carefully market themselves using ancient-sounding vocabulary—"Yoni" for vulva, "Lingam" for penis—while advertising group instruction in massage techniques that would otherwise be recognized as adult sexual education. Participants pay premium fees to attend "sensually charged environments" where they practice intimate methods on each other, all while being told they are accessing "powerful God energy" and achieving "greater connection with cosmic consciousness."

If someone wishes to receive education in sexual massage techniques or attend an adult retreat focused on erotic exploration, that's a perfectly legitimate choice deserving no judgment. The issue isn't the activities themselves—it's the spiritual claims wrapped around them. When these practices are removed from their authentic traditional context, stripped of the ego dissolution and rigorous discipline they originally required, they become something entirely different. Rather than spiritual transformation, they fuel the very lust and ego-desire that genuine spiritual practice seeks to dissolve.

Authentic practices from these traditions required complete absence of personal desire during practice—practitioners approached these techniques without pleasure-seeking agenda, using them as methods for transcending physical attachment rather than enhancing it. The modern retreat version inverts this entirely, encouraging participants to amplify sensual experience while claiming spiritual benefits that have nothing to do with the activities being performed.

The retreat format provides perfect cover for this rebranding, allowing organizers to charge spiritual prices for what might otherwise be recognized as elaborate adult education. Exotic locations, ceremonial language, and mystical framing transform group sexual exploration into something that appears spiritually profound rather than recreational. Participants leave believing they've undergone spiritual initiation when they've essentially attended an expensive intimacy workshop with cosmic marketing.

The Luxury Trap

Both examples reveal how the retreat format itself can become a spiritual trap. The comfort, exclusivity, and high investment required create psychological pressure to find the experience meaningful, regardless of the actual content delivered. Participants who have paid thousands of dollars and traveled to beautiful locations become invested in validating their choice, interpreting even problematic experiences as somehow transformative or necessary for their growth.

The retreat industry has essentially created a premium marketplace for unqualified teachers to access vulnerable seekers under optimal conditions—away from their support systems, in altered states of consciousness, surrounded by the mystique of spiritual authority. When things go wrong, participants are often left to process the aftermath alone, with nowhere to turn for accountability or recourse.

The Absence of Gatekeepers

This lack of accountability isn't an oversight—it's a feature of an industry that has deliberately avoided regulation. Unlike virtually every other field involving human psychology and altered states of consciousness, the spiritual wellness industry operates in a regulatory vacuum that makes the retreat abuses described above not only possible, but inevitable. To understand the contrast, consider medical licensing: physicians must complete four years of medical school followed by at least one year of accredited training. The licensing process itself takes months due to extensive background checks and credential verification. Once licensed, they face continuing education requirements, regular renewals, and state boards that can investigate complaints or revoke licenses for misconduct.

In the spiritual wellness world, oversight is largely voluntary and toothless. Yoga Alliance, perhaps the most recognized credentialing organization for yoga teachers, is often mistaken for a regulatory body. It's not. It's a private nonprofit that provides voluntary registration for teachers who meet their standards— standards that include no competency testing, no background checks, and no mechanism for investigating complaints about teacher misconduct. Registration simply means a teacher completed a recognized training program; it makes no claims about their skill, wisdom, or safety.

Breath-work, despite its potential to induce powerful psychological and physiological states, has no regulatory oversight whatsoever. Practitioners can facilitate sessions that might trigger trauma responses or dissociative episodes with no required training in mental health, no liability insurance mandates, and no professional body to address complaints when things go wrong.

This regulatory vacuum creates a landscape where accountability exists only at the individual level. If a spiritual teacher causes harm—through inappropriate relationships, psychological manipulation, or dangerous practices—there's often no professional body to appeal to, no license to revoke, no standardized process for addressing grievances.

The One-Size-Fits-All Delusion

Perhaps more fundamental than the lack of oversight is the assumption underlying modern certification culture: that the profound complexity of human spiritual development can be reduced to standardized packages, transmitted like software updates, with healing following predictable protocols regardless of the recipient.

This approach treats the mysteries of consciousness as if they were automotive repair—learn the right techniques, follow the proper steps, and transformation will reliably occur. But there's a crucial distinction to be made here. Certain established spiritual traditions do indeed follow systematic approaches to spiritual transcendence and these methodologies have proven effective across centuries. The difference lies not in whether spirituality can involve systematic elements, but in how these systems were developed and how they account for human complexity.

Traditional systems work precisely because they emerged from experienced masters who spent lifetimes observing how different practices affected different types of people. These lineages developed systematic approaches *through* deep understanding of human variability, not despite it. Their methodologies include careful progression, built-in safeguards, and nuanced recognition of psychological and energetic processes—all refined through centuries of real-world application with thousands of diverse students.

The problem isn't systematic approaches to spirituality—it's superficially trained teachers attempting to replicate these sophisticated systems without understanding their underlying principles. Every human being carries a unique constellation of psychological wounds, cultural conditioning, and life experiences. What opens one person's heart might traumatize another. What provides grounding for some might trigger dissociation in others. The same breathing technique that creates blissful states for one participant might precipitate a panic attack in someone with unresolved trauma.

Traditional spiritual lineages understood this complexity intimately. The ancient gurukula system combined academic learning with moral and spiritual growth through years of personal mentorship. Students lived with their teacher in ashram-like settings, learning not only techniques but also life skills, discipline, and values. From initiation until age twenty-five, individuals remained under their teacher's direct guidance, allowing the guru to observe each student's unique temperament, challenges, and capacities over extended periods.

This intimate, long-term relationship enabled experienced teachers to customize their guidance to each student's specific needs. They could observe how different practices affected different personalities, which students needed firmer boundaries and which required gentler encouragement, who was ready for advanced techniques and who needed years more preparation. They witnessed their students' patterns of resistance, their moments of breakthrough, their ways of avoiding difficult truths. The systematic approach emerged from this deep, individualized understanding.

In contrast, modern certification programs treat students like interchangeable units. A weekend training might have fifty participants, each with vastly different backgrounds, traumas, and needs, all receiving identical instruction. The systematic element remains, but stripped of the wisdom that made traditional systems effective. The subtle art of reading a student's readiness, of knowing when to push and when to hold back, of recognizing the signs of spiritual emergency—these skills require years to develop and can't be transmitted through manuals or workshops.

More concerning is how this assembly-line approach handles advanced practices. In established traditions, the more powerful techniques—those that can dramatically alter consciousness or move substantial amounts of energy through the system—are transmitted only after years of preparation. A seasoned teacher ensures that a student's body, mind, and energy system have been properly conditioned to handle the intense experiences these practices can generate. The systematic progression exists precisely to prepare students for what comes next.

Weekend certification programs, however, sometimes include these advanced techniques without foundational preparation or proper context. A newly certified teacher might learn a powerful breathwork pattern or energetic practice without understanding the prerequisites their students need, or the signs that someone isn't ready for such intensity. They may inadvertently guide unprepared individuals into states their nervous systems aren't equipped to integrate, not out of malice but from simply not knowing what they don't know.

The Performance of Authority

The ego, fed by new authority and the intoxicating rush of being seen as "awakened," often rushes to fill gaps in understanding with performance. The newly certified teacher begins to play the part of the enlightened one, modeling borrowed wisdom and curated compassion while their own inner work remains unfinished. They speak in spiritual clichés, adopt the mannerisms of teachers they admire, and learn to hold space for others while their own psychological material stays unprocessed.

This performance can be convincing, even to themselves. They've memorized the right phrases: "Hold space," "Trust the process," "Everything happens for a reason." They've cultivated the right aesthetic: flowing clothes, meaningful jewelry, a knowing smile that suggests they've seen beyond the veil. They've even developed the right energy: calm, centered, mysteriously wise. But beneath the performance, the same patterns of ego, insecurity, and unprocessed material continue to run the show.

This phenomenon thrives because the demand for teachers outpaces the supply of seasoned masters. People are hungry for guidance, for someone to hold the lantern while they navigate their own darkness. Traditional lineages that once produced mature teachers operated on different timelines—decades of preparation for a handful of true masters. But consumer culture demands instant gratification, and spiritual consumer culture follows suit.

The industry obliges, but in obliging, it commodifies. Programs are marketed as gateways to purpose and income simultaneously, promising not just personal growth but a ready-made career in helping others grow. The deeper traditions from which these practices originate are often trimmed, simplified, or stripped of their philosophical and cultural roots to fit a business model that needs to produce certified practitioners on a predictable schedule.

At the core of this lies a very human tendency to seek validation, and teaching provides a particularly potent form. For some, the role becomes the ultimate stage upon which the ego can perform: receiving admiration, confessions, even worship. Students bow, share their deepest secrets, hang on every word. The teacher becomes the center of a small universe of adoration.

Here the danger crystallizes—not in the absence of knowledge alone, but in the presence of power without self-mastery. The newly certified teacher may start with good intentions, but the seductive pull of being seen as wise or special can gradually corrupt even sincere motivations. They begin to believe their own press. They mistake their students' projections for their own realization. They confuse the ability to induce experiences in others with their own spiritual development.

The old traditions had gatekeepers for good reason. They understood that the urge to teach often arises from the very ego that spiritual work is meant to transcend. They knew that power corrupts, especially the subtle power of spiritual authority. They built in safeguards: long apprenticeships, rigorous testing, communities that could provide feedback and accountability.

In modern certification culture, these safeguards have largely evaporated, replaced by market forces that reward confidence over competence, charisma over depth, and speed over thoroughness. The result is a spiritual landscape populated by well-meaning but under-prepared teachers, each carrying a certificate that says they're qualified to guide others through territories they've barely begun to explore themselves.

The most troubling aspect of this system isn't the obvious failures—the unprepared teachers or inadequate training programs—but something more subtle and dangerous. It's when sincere seekers, those who have genuinely touched something transformative, become unconscious merchants of their own spiritual memories. These are not calculating deceivers but well-meaning souls who mistake a single profound experience for permanent wisdom, a glimpse of truth for graduation into its guardianship.

The real danger lies in the ego's remarkable ability to colonize even the most sacred experiences. What begins as genuine spiritual experience becomes the foundation for spiritual performance, transforming humble servants of truth into unwitting guardians of illusion. To understand how this happens—how the very experiences meant to dissolve the separate self become its most sophisticated disguise—we need to follow two seekers whose genuine encounters with the sacred gradually crystallized into something far more treacherous: the unconscious performance of enlightenment itself.

The Lantern Bearers

Deep in the carnival's shadows, where the main thoroughfare twisted into forgotten alleys, two seekers found their moment of truth within different tents on the same moonless night.

Darius emerged from the Vine of Visions tent, his legs unsteady beneath him, reality still soft around the edges like watercolors bleeding into rain. Fifteen years of climbing corporate ladders — the quarterly reports, performance metrics, strategic planning sessions — dissolved in eight hours of ayahuasca revelation. The vine had torn through every boundary he'd ever known, and he'd understood with crushing clarity that everything was sacred, interconnected, perfect.

The tent keeper pressed a small cloth bundle into his trembling hands. "Integration," she whispered. "The real work begins now."

Three tents away, Luna stumbled from the House of Sacred Breath, her chest cracked open like morning sky after storm. A decade of chronic pain — doctor after specialist, procedure after failed procedure — had driven her to the breath-work tent in desperation. But something ancient and knotted in her ribs had simply... released. The agony dissolved like salt in deep water. More than healing: as breath moved through her, she'd felt herself expanding beyond skin, becoming the tent, the other participants, the very air they shared.

The breath keeper placed gentle hands on Luna's shoulders. "You've remembered who you are," he said. "Now you must decide what to do with that remembering."

Both wandered the carnival paths that night, transformed, carrying the same burning question: How do I live with this truth? How do I serve what I've seen?

By dawn, the answer found them.

***

A week later, Darius discovered the certification tent — canvas painted with vines and sacred geometry. "Teachers of the Path - Certification in Sacred Guidance."

56

The woman behind the low table wore white linen that caught amber light. Her smile was knowing. "You've touched something profound," she said before Darius spoke. "The question is: will you share it with those still wandering in darkness?"

"Our intensive transforms authentic experience into skilled guidance. Seven days to learn foundational practices, plus one evening on holding sacred space."

Darius felt his chest tighten with recognition. This was his purpose crystallizing. Of course he was meant to guide others.

Still, something nagged. "Only seven days? The carnival healers seem to have trained for decades."

Her laugh was silver bells. "Those old practitioners cling to outdated methods. Consciousness has evolved. What once took decades can now be transmitted in intensive immersion. Besides," she leaned forward, "you already carry the wisdom. We're simply helping you remember how to share it."

Luna found similar promises at the Breath Temple. The facilitator sat surrounded by students hanging on his every word.

"Knowledge without application is merely spiritual entertainment. Who among you will answer the call to become bridges themselves?"

When Luna approached afterward, his eyes softened. "I remember your session—such beautiful opening. Our ten-day intensive covers everything: techniques, safety protocols, integration support."

"Ten days?" Luna asked, thinking of the weathered masters who seemed to carry decades of wisdom in their presence.

"The breath itself is the teacher," he explained smoothly. "Our role is simply to hold space and trust the process. The most important qualification is having done deep work—which you clearly have."

Both signed up that week, drawn not just by purpose but by the promise of remaining in the spiritual bubble that had become their world.

***

The intensives compressed years of wisdom into intensive weeks. Darius learned breathing techniques, ceremonial protocols, integration frameworks. He practiced holding space for emotional releases and received "Sacred Emergency Response"—a slim manual covering everything from panic attacks to spiritual crises in bullet-pointed brevity.

During role-play scenarios, Darius noticed how quickly they moved through complex situations. "What if someone completely dissociates?"

"Trust the process and your intuition," came the reply. "Plant consciousness will guide you."

The answer felt profound yet vaguely unsatisfying, but Darius dismissed his doubt. He was overthinking—the same analytical mind that had trapped him before awakening.

Luna's breath-work training covered trauma release and psychological safety in compressed modules. When she asked about severe PTSD, the instructor nodded sagely: "The breath knows what it's doing. Trust whatever emerges."

Both received certificates and registration with the carnival's Registry of Sacred Teachers. Neither questioned what oversight this provided; the certificates felt official, legitimate.

What they didn't realize: their instructors had completed similar intensives just months earlier. The lineages they'd joined were shallow streams, not deep wells—chains of recently certified teachers training others in techniques they'd barely mastered themselves.

***

Four months later, their tents appeared on the carnival's edges.

Darius "Sacred Psychology - Integration for the Awakened Soul" drew Viktor, a software engineer whose anxiety was eating him alive, whose successful career felt like a beautiful prison.

"Plant medicines revealed that anxiety is the soul crying out for its true home," Darius explained, his voice taking ceremony's measured cadence. "Your system rejects the artificial matrix because it remembers what's real. This resistance is sacred—calling you back to yourself."

Viktor felt something unknot in his chest. Finally, someone who understood the restlessness.

Luna's "Temple of Breath - Healing Through Sacred Air" attracted Yuki, drowning in postpartum depression that muffled every color in her world.

"Breath-work releases trauma stored not just in your body, but your ancestral line," Luna explained. "Sometimes we carry our mothers' pain, our grandmothers' grief. Today, we break those cycles."

Both felt genuinely called to serve. In those early months, their guidance seemed blessed—clients left lighter, clearer, more hopeful.

Word spread through hidden pathways. Testimonials accumulated like offerings at tent entrances. Both felt the warm glow of confirmation: they were serving, healing, channeling divine will through the carnival's sacred grounds.

Success bred devotion. Within a year, both attracted not just clients but disciples—dedicated souls who considered them spiritual parents, arranging themselves like planets orbiting their sun.

Darius' inner circle: three women who managed his schedule with protective care, screened clients for "readiness," and had absorbed his language so completely that conversations felt like speaking with extensions of his consciousness.

Luna's devoted followers numbered six—seekers who called her "Sacred Mother" and vied to demonstrate their devotion, their worthiness to serve her mission.

Both groups developed their own dialects: carnival terminology mixed with ancient-sounding phrases and vocabulary their teachers had coined. When family members expressed concern about devotion's intensity, both circles had ready explanations: "Those who haven't done deep work feel triggered by transformation." "The unawakened mind resists what it cannot understand."

Neither Darius nor Luna questioned the adoration. Of course those touched by truth would recognize light-carriers. Of course healing created gratitude.

***

Viktor had been Darius' regular for eighteen months when questions began nibbling at his certainty. Initially, he'd found genuine peace. Darius' validation of his spiritual hunger had been medicine after years of feeling insane for wanting more than success.

But something shifted. Darius' interpretations became increasingly ornate and absolute. A difficult work week wasn't stress—it was "the old paradigm's death throes as your soul calls you home." Relationship struggles weren't human complexity— they were "the universe testing your commitment to awakening."

More troubling was Darius' response to questioning. What had been gentle guidance now carried sharp edges. "I'm sensing deep ego resistance, Viktor. This is precisely what we need to explore."

Viktor found himself apologizing for having doubts, for not immediately seeing truth through Darius' eyes. The dynamic had shifted: Darius was no longer helping him explore insights, but interpreting Viktor's reality for him.

The breaking point arrived during group ceremony. Viktor shared that his anxiety was genuinely improving—through their work, yes, but also through practical changes like better sleep, exercise, work boundaries. Darius' response froze his blood:

"Viktor, I invite you to look beneath the surface story your ego is crafting. The mind loves claiming credit for healing, but what we're witnessing is your soul finally accepting our sacred work's gifts. These external changes are merely reflections of inner transformation."

The devoted circle nodded like flowers following sun. Viktor felt something cold pierce his chest. His own experience was being revised, his agency dissolved, his understanding corrected by someone whose primary qualification was confidence wrapped in ceremony.

After the session, Viktor approached privately. "I'm grateful for everything you've shared, but I think it's time to continue independently."

Darius' face cycled through surprise, hurt, then something colder. "Of course, Viktor. Sometimes souls need distance when work reaches deepest layers. The ego has infinite strategies for avoiding dissolution." His smile was understanding, but his eyes held winter. "The tent remains open when you're ready to surrender more completely."

Viktor tried finding accountability. The Registry of Sacred Teachers maintained directories, not oversight. They suggested contacting Darius' training lineage—a chain of recently certified teachers with no master practitioner taking responsibility.

The contrast with traditional healers was stark. Weathered practitioners who'd trained for decades had clear lineages with accountability structures. But certification culture had created credentials without oversight, authority without responsibility.

Viktor departed the carnival entirely. Darius registered his leaving only as confirmation: Viktor wasn't prepared for deeper mysteries. Some seekers had more ego investment than others. Viktor had received what he could integrate—anything more would have overwhelmed his system.

Darius' inner circle gathered like protective spirits. "He wasn't willing to do real work," one observed. "Some people want healing without transformation," offered another. Darius felt understood, validated.

***

Luna's reckoning arrived on a humid evening when the carnival air hung thick as sap.

Carmen had been coming to Luna's tent for months—a gentle soul carrying childhood wounds like stones in her chest. During their regular breath-work session, something shifted. Carmen's breathing pattern escalated beyond the familiar rhythms of release. Her body began to shake, not with the trembling of emotional breakthrough but with violent convulsions that made the tent walls seem to pulse.

Luna watched Carmen's breathing deepen, her body beginning to shake with the familiar tremors of emotional release. But when Carmen tried to slow her breath, to ground herself, Luna gently guided her back to the pattern.

"Don't retreat now," Luna whispered. "Your system is ready to release what it's carried for decades. Just breathe through the resistance."

Carmen's eyes flickered with uncertainty, but she trusted Luna's guidance. The breathing intensified. Memories began surfacing— fractured images, body sensations, emotions without context. Carmen's breath became ragged, panicked.

"I need to stop," Carmen gasped between breaths. "Something's happening—"

"That's the breakthrough approaching," Luna assured her, believing completely in what her training had taught: the breath

was infinitely wise, incapable of harm. "Let the ancient trauma surface. Your nervous system knows how to heal itself."

Luna encouraged deeper breathing, longer holds, more intensity. Carmen's body began to convulse as suppressed memories flooded her system—but without any tools to process the overwhelming surge of traumatic material. The oxygen-rich state amplified everything: terror, rage, helplessness, all magnified beyond her capacity to integrate.

Carmen's consciousness fragmented under the assault. Her breath froze in a semi-conscious state, caught between the hyper-oxygenation of the technique and the protective shutdown of an overwhelmed nervous system. She remained suspended in this liminal space for nearly an hour, neither fully present nor completely absent.

When Carmen finally returned to ordinary awareness, her eyes held a distant, shattered quality that made Luna's stomach clench with sudden doubt.

For days afterward, Carmen moved through the carnival like a ghost. Simple conversations became impossible. She'd start sentences and lose the thread, her attention scattering like leaves in wind. The breath-work had cracked open traumas her psyche wasn't prepared to process, leaving her floating in dissociated fragments.

She never returned to Luna's tent. Within weeks, concerned practitioners whispered through the healing circles: Luna's methods had pushed someone beyond their threshold, leaving them unmoored from their own life.

When other practitioners approached Luna with gentle concerns, her Sacred Mothers encircled her like protective spirits. Their explanations flowed like silk over steel: "Carmen's soul called forth exactly what she needed to release." "Sometimes healing looks like shattering before wholeness." "The feminine mysteries work in ways the rational mind cannot comprehend."

Luna found herself nodding along. Yes, Carmen had touched something primal, perhaps too quickly. Not everyone's nervous system could handle such rapid purification. Some souls required gentler approaches, slower unfolding. It wasn't Luna's fault—it was simply Carmen's rhythm of healing, intense and mysterious as birth itself.

The interpretation felt both comforting and true. Luna had been called to midwife deep transformation, and like any birth, the process could appear chaotic to untrained eyes. Those who questioned her methods simply hadn't developed the sensitivity to recognize profound healing in its raw, unpolished form.

Her remaining circle absorbed this wisdom like rain on desert sand. Carmen became their cautionary tale of what happened when someone accessed powerful medicine without proper surrender. They spoke of her with compassionate sadness—a sister who'd touched the threshold of liberation but couldn't cross it. Anyone who questioned Luna's guidance after that was gently redirected: "Even Carmen's experience served the collective healing. Some souls volunteer to show us the edges of what's possible."

***

Years flowed like honey in the carnival's timeless atmosphere. Both teachers expanded, their followings deepened, their certainty crystallized into something harder than diamond. They became featured attractions—speaking at main stages, leading intensive retreats, appearing in newsletters as examples of authentic awakening.

The early doubts about preparation had been smoothly integrated into mythology. They hadn't needed extensive training because they were naturals, chosen vessels, souls who'd incarnated specifically to serve awakening. Their profound experiences were qualification enough; additional training would have cluttered pure transmission with unnecessary concepts.

Other seekers still wandered pathways, driven by the same hunger that had once brought Darius and Luna to their first transformative tents. But the teachers had forgotten their own pilgrimage, forgotten the humility of those first stumbling steps into mystery.

Their lanterns burned with steady flames, casting dancing shadows on canvas walls, illuminating everything except the truth: they had long ago stopped walking the path they claimed to guide. They had become performers of awakening rather than practitioners, merchants of transformation rather than embodiments.

The ego, fed by endless reverence and the intoxicating nectar of being needed, had learned to wear their genuine experiences like elaborate costumes. They performed enlightenment so convincingly that even they believed the theater, mistaking memory of truth for truth itself, echo of awakening for awakening, role of teacher for wisdom's reality.

In rare quiet moments—when tents emptied, seekers departed, carnival sounds faded—something would stir in each. A memory of that first night, that first glimpse, that first crack in ordinary awareness. But the noise of their success, constant demand for guidance, the weight of others' projections and desperate hopes, had grown too loud.

The whisper was easily dismissed as doubt, as ego's final gambit to sabotage sacred service. And so the performance continued, night after night, under eternal carnival lights, where the most dangerous lost guides are never conscious predators stalking the vulnerable, but wanderers who mistook a single footstep for the entire journey—souls who glimpsed the mountain peak once and built careers teaching others how to climb while still standing at base camp.

The truth they'd touched still pulsed beneath the surface, still called to every genuine seeker who entered their tents. But each night of performance buried it deeper—authentic experience fossilizing into rehearsed wisdom, living insight crystallizing into dead certainty. They had become cartographers drawing maps of territories they'd never fully explored, lighthouse keepers whose own beacon had long since burned out, leaving them to guide ships through darkness they could no longer navigate themselves.

Their tents glowed warmly in the carnival night, beautiful and mysterious as ever, drawing seekers like moths to flame. But what waited inside was no longer the living truth that had first cracked them open—only its elaborate impersonation, performed by those who had forgotten the difference between pointing at the moon and claiming to be it.

Now, let's step back from Darius and Luna's tents and examine what we've just witnessed—because this is perhaps the most insidious trap in the entire carnival, precisely because it begins with something genuine.

Darius and Luna weren't con artists. They didn't set out to deceive anyone. Their initial experiences were real—the ayahuasca ceremony genuinely cracked Darius open, Luna's breath-work session authentically released years of trapped pain. These weren't fabricated spiritual experiences or clever marketing ploys. They touched something true, profound, transformative.

But here's where the trap springs: they mistook a single experience for mastery, a glimpse for graduation, a personal healing for universal wisdom. The same ego that spiritual work is meant to dissolve simply adapted, learning new vocabulary and putting on different robes. Instead of continuing their own journey with humility, they appointed themselves guides for others walking similar paths.

The carnival's certification tents made this transition feel legitimate, even noble. "Turn your awakening into service," they whispered. "Share your gifts with those still suffering." The programs were brief enough to maintain transformation's high, elaborate enough to feel substantial, and profitable enough to solve the practical problem of making a living while staying within the spiritual bubble.

Notice how the language evolved. Darius went from experiencing personal healing to declaring "Plant medicines revealed that anxiety is the soul crying out for its true home." Luna shifted from finding relief to proclaiming "Breath-work releases trauma stored not just in your body, but your ancestral line." Personal became universal, subjective became objective, temporary became permanent. This isn't conscious deception—it's the ego's natural tendency to colonize any experience and claim ownership over mystery itself.

The followers who gathered around them weren't stupid or weak. They were genuine seekers attracted to the same energy that had once drawn Darius and Luna to their own teachers. But they were receiving secondhand wisdom—interpretations of experiences rather than direct encounters, maps drawn by people who'd visited the territory once and now claimed expertise in every trail.

The inner circles formed organically because Darius and Luna needed validation that their interpretations were correct, their methods effective, their insights profound. Surrounding themselves with people who reflected their certainty back created closed loops where doubt became "ego resistance" and questioning became "not being ready for the work."

This pattern repeats throughout the carnival because it feels so righteous. Unlike obvious charlatans, these teachers offer something that was once real. They've simply forgotten that pointing toward the moon isn't the same as being the moon, that having touched truth once doesn't make you its permanent ambassador.

The most insidious aspect of this trap is how it corrupts genuine spiritual experiences. Darius and Luna's initial awakenings were valid—they did touch something transformative. But instead of remaining humble students of those mysteries, they graduated themselves and opened schools. They stopped being seekers and started being finders. They ceased walking the path and began selling maps to places they'd visited once, long ago.

What makes this phenomenon particularly tragic is how it exploits the very structures we examined earlier—the certification assembly line, the absence of oversight, the one-size-fits-all mentality. These systemic problems don't create Darius and Luna; they simply provide perfect conditions for their unconscious deception to flourish and spread.

The carnival is full of such souls—well-meaning people who had real breakthrough experiences and then built identities around those moments instead of allowing them to dissolve the very ego that now claims ownership over enlightenment. They are sincere in their delusion, convinced they serve the light while casting shadows they cannot see.

Authentic guides do exist, though they operate far from the carnival's noise and spectacle. These are the lineage holders—teachers who received their understanding through decades of rigorous training under established masters, who carry wisdom that has been refined and tested across generations. They exist within living traditions that maintain standards, accountability, and depth that weekend certifications cannot replicate.

Such teachers often remain largely invisible to casual seekers, working within communities that understand the slow, demanding nature of genuine spiritual development. When they do teach, they focus on cultivating qualities that Darius and Luna have abandoned: discernment over blind faith, inner authority over external dependence, direct experience over borrowed insights. They understand that their role is to make themselves unnecessary —to guide students toward their own unshakeable knowing rather than creating followers who need constant validation and interpretation.

These masters recognize that authentic spiritual development requires the same dedication as mastering any profound discipline. They know the difference between peak experiences and integrated wisdom, between temporary states and stable transformation, between touching truth once and embodying it consistently. Most importantly, they understand their own limitations and remain students themselves within their chosen lineages.

Such teachers rarely have the shiniest tents or the biggest followings. They've made peace with being ordinary human beings who happen to have spent time exploring consciousness. They remember that every teacher remains forever a student, that wisdom often wears work clothes rather than ceremonial robes, and that the most profound truths resist packaging for mass consumption.

But here's the challenge: even this description could become another spiritual checklist, another way the seeking mind tries to guarantee safety in an inherently uncertain territory. The same psychological patterns that created Darius and Luna can co-opt any criteria we establish for authentic teaching. Humility can be performed, uncertainty can be feigned, ordinariness can become its own form of spiritual pride.

This is perhaps the carnival's cruelest irony: the very experiences that could liberate us from ego become the ego's most sophisticated costume. The same awakening that could teach us surrender becomes the foundation for spiritual pride. The mystical insights meant to dissolve the separate self become evidence of how special and advanced we are.

Darius and Luna's tents will continue glowing in the carnival night, attracting seekers who hunger for what they once authentically tasted. Some visitors will find genuine healing—even flawed guides can occasionally point toward real territory. But the tragedy remains: two souls who glimpsed the infinite allowed that glimpse to become another prison, trading the living adventure of awakening for the static role of teacher.

The lantern bearers shine their lights into the carnival darkness, believing themselves illuminated. But they cannot see that their flames no longer burn with the fire they first received—only with the reflection of that fire in the eyes of those who still believe they are ablaze.

Epilogue: The Eternal Return

Somewhere in the carnival's endless night, another seeker stumbles from a tent with tears streaming down her face, reality still trembling around her like heat waves. She has touched something vast and luminous, something that exploded every assumption about herself and the world. For the first time in her life, she knows with absolute certainty that everything is connected, that love is the fabric of existence, that she is not separate from anything or anyone.

By morning, the certification tent has appeared in her peripheral vision. By next week, she will sign up for the teacher training. By next month, her own tent will glow warmly at the carnival's edge, drawing seekers who recognize in her presence the same unmistakable glow that once drew Darius and Luna to their first transformative experiences.

The cycle turns. The wheel spins. The carnival continues its eternal dance between awakening and delusion, between truth and its performance, between the pathless path and the comfortable cage of spiritual certainty.

And in the deep silence beneath all the carnival's noise— beneath the testimonials and teachings, the certifications and ceremonies, the seeking and finding—the real mystery remains untouched, unowned, forever pointing toward itself with a humor and compassion that embraces even its most elaborate impersonations.

The truth needs no teachers, no tents, no tickets for admission. It offers itself freely to every open heart, as available in this moment as it was in Darius and Luna's first glimpse, as present in the doubts of departing students as in the certainty of devoted followers.

The lantern bearers of sincere delusion serve this truth too, in their own unknowing way—by showing us exactly what happens when we mistake the reflection for the source, the map for the territory, the finger pointing at the moon for the moon itself.

Their tents remain open. Their followers remain devoted. Their performances continue with conviction so complete it becomes another kind of teaching—a demonstration of how the ego can hijack even the most sacred experiences and use them to rebuild the very prison that spiritual work was meant to dissolve.

The carnival spins on through the endless night, offering every possible variation on the ancient human drama of losing and finding ourselves, of mistaking experiences for identity, of confusing temporary openings for permanent attainments. And in that spinning, in that endless cycling between clarity and confusion, between seeing and blindness, the deepest teaching emerges:

Perhaps the real awakening isn't in transcending this dance between truth and delusion, but in recognizing it so clearly that we're no longer caught by either side. Perhaps wisdom isn't in avoiding the trap of spiritual pride, but in seeing through it so completely that even falling into it becomes another opportunity to laugh at the magnificent absurdity of being human seekers in an infinite mystery that was never actually hidden.

Darius and Luna's tents glow on in the carnival night—beautiful, tragic, and perfectly necessary reminders that even our most sincere delusions serve the awakening that needs no lanterns because it is the light by which all lanterns burn.

The carnival continues. The seekers wander. The mystery remains.

And somewhere in the shadows between the tents, beyond all teachers and teachings, the truth that was never lost continues to call to every heart that has forgotten it was never separate from what it seeks.

5

Cults: The Altar of Ego

In the deeper reaches of the spiritual carnival, beyond the fortune tellers and crystal healers, beyond even the earnest teachers offering their weekend workshops, lies territory entirely different from what we've encountered. Here, the tents give way to permanent structures—compounds built from the accumulated devotion and resources of those who didn't just visit the carnival, but never left.

What begins as a quest for personal guidance can, in these shadowed corners, morph into something far more insidious: the cult. The solitary teacher expands their influence, drawing followers into webs of collective devotion that promise enlightenment but deliver control. The spiritual marketplace, with its hungry seekers and vulnerable hearts, becomes fertile ground for predators who understand that the very qualities that make someone genuinely spiritual—openness, willingness to surrender ego, trust in guidance—can be weaponized against them.

These are the domains of those who style themselves as spiritual authorities—masters, leaders, teachers, mentors, gurus, guides, spiritual directors—figures who have claimed positions of ultimate guidance over communities of seekers. The statistics tell a sobering story: research suggests that between 0.5% to 3% of individuals are involved in a cult at some point in their lifetime, while estimates indicate there are between 3,000 to 5,000 destructive groups operating in the United States alone. These aren't remote monasteries or obvious fringe movements—they operate through wellness centers, yoga studios, online programs, retreat facilities, or religious communities, often incorporating legitimate practices like meditation, breathwork, and bodywork, but bending these tools toward psychological control rather than genuine liberation.

To understand what we encounter in these shadowed territories, we must first honor what spiritual authority represents at its highest expression. The word "guru" emerges from the Sanskrit roots gu (darkness) and ru (dispeller)—one who dispels darkness. In traditional contexts, a guru embodies wisdom, compassion, and selfless service, existing not to accumulate power but to illuminate the inherent divinity within each student. The genuine guru's ultimate success is measured not by the loyalty they command but by the spiritual sovereignty they help students achieve.

This sacred relationship has been recognized across wisdom traditions—whether in Christian hermitages, Buddhist monasteries, yogic ashrams, or indigenous tribes. The genuine spiritual authority serves a consistent function: holding space for another's awakening while pointing always toward the student's own inner knowing.

The crucial distinction cuts to the heart of everything: a cult leader is not a guru in any meaningful sense, despite appropriating the title and trappings of spiritual authority. Where the true guru seeks to make themselves dispensable, the cult leader makes themselves indispensable. Where the mature master cultivates independence, the false master cultivates dependency. Where genuine spiritual authority empowers the student to eventually transcend external guidance, the predatory leader ensures that liberation remains forever just beyond reach, contingent upon continued submission.

The modern wellness industry—a trillion-dollar ecosystem of retreats, trainings, and transformational experiences—has created unprecedented opportunities for such figures to flourish. They speak the language of ancient wisdom but operate with sophisticated manipulation techniques. Cult expert Steven Hassan's BITE Model identifies four overlapping categories of control: Behavior, Information, Thought, and Emotional manipulation— tactics that these spiritual predators have refined to an art form.

74

They understand that people arriving at their doors aren't just seeking spiritual insight; they're seeking healing from trauma, meaning in a chaotic world, community in an isolated society, and often a parent figure to guide them when life feels overwhelming. This vulnerability isn't weakness—it's human. The desire for transcendence, for growth, for connection to something greater represents some of our highest aspirations. But predators have learned to recognize and exploit these noble hungers.

The recruitment process targets people during vulnerable transitions: divorce, job loss, death of loved ones, spiritual crisis, or the modern epidemic of meaninglessness. The initial contact feels like destiny—a teaching that speaks directly to deepest pain, a community that sees and appreciates you in ways the outside world never has. What follows is gradual psychological reformation. Boundaries dissolve under the guise of spiritual openness. Critical thinking becomes reframed as ego resistance. Financial resources flow toward the group in ever-increasing amounts—first as donations, then as investments in spiritual development, finally as proof of commitment to the path.

The master maintains control through intermittent reinforcement, alternating between love-bombing and magnifying followers' insecurities. This manipulation employs three core behaviors that define traumatizing narcissists: intimidation, belittling, and humiliation—recast in Orwellian fashion as necessary means toward spiritual purification. Social connections outside the group are gradually portrayed as obstacles to growth, sources of negative energy that threaten spiritual progress.

These dynamics employ systematic deception, compartmentalized information, loaded language that stops critical thinking, and the installation of phobias around questioning or leaving. The master becomes the sole interpreter of inner experience, the ultimate authority on what feelings mean and what actions should follow. They position themselves as the gatekeeper between followers and enlightenment, ensuring that spiritual progress depends entirely on their approval and presence.

The psychology is as predictable as it is dangerous. Leaders often embody the dark triad—narcissism, Machiavellianism, psychopathy—viewing followers not as equals on a path but as extensions of their own ego. Sexual boundary violations are common, framed as "tantric healing," "sacred sexuality," or necessary initiation into deeper teachings. Physical control manifests through extreme dietary restrictions, exhaustion from excessive work requirements, and isolation in controlled environments where normal reality checks become impossible.

The psychological toll is immense. Former members commonly report dissociation, depression, anxiety, financial ruin, and a shattered ability to trust their own judgment. Research shows they experience an extended "in-between time" after leaving—a chaotic period of reorganizing themselves and finding new perspective, often involving self-harm, suicide attempts, or substance abuse. Recovery involves learning to recognize chronic dysregulation states and developing self-compassion after years of self-alienation.

Yet these groups persist because they offer something real alongside the manipulation: community, purpose, practices that can genuinely produce altered states and meaningful experiences, and the temporary relief of surrendering difficult life decisions. The tragedy is that all of these legitimate needs could be met through healthy spiritual communities that empower rather than enslave their members.

The difference between authentic spiritual guidance and cult leadership lies in the direction the relationship points. A true teacher directs you toward your own inner authority, your own capacity for wisdom, your own relationship with the sacred. They may challenge your ego and push you beyond comfort zones—but always with the goal of strengthening your ability to navigate life independently. The false master directs you toward themselves, making themselves indispensable to your spiritual life and creating dependency rather than empowerment.

Not all group spiritual experiences are cults. Genuine communities encourage critical thinking and autonomy, welcome questions, and support members' connections to family and friends outside the group. But the line blurs when reverence tips into worship, when questions are punished, and when the group's "truth" overrides personal intuition. In the carnival, these enclaves lurk at the edges, away from the flashy tents, their glow drawing in the weary like moths to flames that consume rather than illuminate.

In the story that follows, we'll witness this process unfold through the experience of someone whose intelligence and spiritual sincerity become the very qualities that make her vulnerable to sophisticated manipulation. We'll see how the promise of transcendence can become a trap that keeps seekers from accessing the freedom that was already theirs to claim. We'll venture into an enclave where charisma builds empires on the backs of devoted disciples, where dependency is manufactured through the systematic exploitation of human longing for connection and meaning.

Most crucially, we'll explore what it takes to recognize when a teacher has become a tyrant, and the inner strength required to reclaim one's light from the shadows that masquerade as illumination.

The Master's Shadow

Alex slowed her steps at the carnival's fringe, where laughter and neon dissolved into hushed corridors of shadow. Here, the air thickened as though silence itself had weight. Lanterns dimmed. The pulse of drums receded until the only sound was the fragile rhythm of her own breath.

At thirty-four, she carried the quiet ache of collapse. A divorce that had stripped her skin raw, friendships eroded into polite distance, a sister—Anya—whose persistent texts she ignored out of shame. Anya had been her anchor once, the only family who had stood by her when the marriage dissolved, but Alex couldn't stomach the concern in her voice. It reminded her of all the ways she had failed. The last voicemail still sat unopened: "Alex, please. I know you're hurting, but disappearing won't fix anything. I love you. Call me back."

But love felt like judgment now. Love meant admitting she'd been wrong about John, wrong about her choices, wrong about everything that had led her to this carnival of desperate seekers. Nights bled into empty mornings, freelance design jobs churned her talent into soulless corporate logos and wedding invitations for other people's happiness. *Something real.* That's what I want. *Something that makes sense of this gray wasteland I'm calling life.*

The amber glow of a lone tent beckoned through the shadows. Its light pulsed like a heartbeat, steady and hypnotic. The sign above its entrance declared: *The Veil of Illumination — For Those Who Seek True Light.*

True light. The words seemed to whisper directly to the hollow space behind her ribs where hope used to live.

The flap shifted. A man emerged—tall, draped in robes that glowed like stars in the night sky, his presence commanding but serene. Mid-forties, perhaps, with salt-and-pepper hair that fell to his shoulders and eyes that seemed to hold depths she couldn't fathom. His gaze fixed on hers with a force that pinned her in place, as if he could see through the careful mask she'd been wearing for months.

"You've been circling," he said, his voice low, steady, with the calm cadence of someone who had rehearsed holiness until it became second nature.

Alex's mouth opened, but no words formed. How could he possibly—she'd only been walking for minutes, hadn't she?

"Looking for what you cannot name," he continued, stepping aside with effortless grace. His movements were fluid, deliberate, each gesture seeming to carry weight and meaning. "The thing that gnaws at you in the small hours. The emptiness that no distraction can fill." His smile was gentle, almost paternal. "Come. The light does not chase—it waits."

Inside, the air was a trap of sandalwood and something darker, bitter, addictive. Frankincense maybe, or myrrh—something ancient and sacred that made her feel small in its presence. Lanterns burned in unnatural stillness, their flames neither flickering nor wavering. Cushions circled a platform draped in silk the color of dried blood. He gestured with one elegant hand, and

Alex sat. The cushion seemed molded to her frame, as though others had already sunk into it with the same trembling vulnerability.

"Why have you come?" His tone was gentle, even compassionate, though his gaze seemed to peel back layers without consent. There was something unsettling about how completely still he was, how his eyes never seemed to blink.

"I..." The words caught in her throat. What was she supposed to say? That her life had fallen apart? That she was drowning in an ocean of her own failures? "I want clarity," she whispered finally. "Something real."

"Clarity," he said, folding his hands with deliberate precision, "is not given. It is uncovered, as a sculptor reveals the figure within the stone. But first..." His eyes seemed to penetrate deeper, and Alex felt exposed, as if he could see every shameful thought she'd ever harbored. "First, you must offer the stone willingly." His smile was soft, almost paternal, but there was something predatory lurking beneath it. "And it requires commitment."

The word *commitment* rang like a command, though his tone remained gentle. Alex nodded despite her chest tightening. Something about the way he said it made it sound less like a choice and more like a requirement for salvation.

His eyes glimmered with satisfaction at her compliance. "I see your wounds," he said, leaning forward slightly. "Your father's absence—the way he chose his bottle over his daughter. Your husband's rejection—how he made you feel like you were never enough, never quite the woman he wanted you to be. Even your sister's voice, which you cannot bear to hear because it reminds you of how far you've fallen."

Alex's pulse stuttered. She hadn't mentioned John or Anya. She was certain she hadn't mentioned her father's drinking. *How does he know?* Doubt stirred, but his phrasing was lyrical, convincing, delivered with such calm certainty that it felt like divine revelation rather than cold reading.

"All these are threads in a pattern of abandonment," he continued, his voice taking on a hypnotic quality. "You suffer not because they left, but because you never left yourself. You cling to the small, frightened child within, feeding her stories of unworthiness. But I see beyond that illusion." He reached out and touched her hand, his fingers cool and dry. "I see the light you've been hiding from yourself."

The touch sent an electric shock through her system—part revulsion, part desperate gratitude. The warmth in his voice pulled at her ribs, convincing her she had been truly seen, perhaps for the first time in her life. This stranger understood her better than John ever had, better than Anya with her worried texts and careful suggestions about therapy.

"What's your name?" she asked, though part of her suspected he might not give real names in places like this.

"Names are constructs of the ego," he said with that same gentle smile. "But you may call me Master Thorne. And you are Alexandra, though you've been hiding behind 'Alex' for so long you've forgotten the power in your full name."

She hadn't told him her name at all.

***

She returned the next day. And the next. His teachings slid between comfort and unease like a blade wrapped in silk. The tent became her sanctuary, the only place where the gray fog of her depression seemed to lift.

"Love is an illusion," he would say during their sessions, eyes half-closed in seeming meditation. "The attachment you call love is merely biological programming designed to keep you trapped in cycles of suffering. But devotion—devotion to truth—endures beyond death, beyond pain, beyond the small concerns of the ego."

The words sounded wise, profound even, but Alex found herself wondering, *Whose truth?* Then he would fix her with that penetrating gaze, and the question would evaporate like morning mist.

Other seekers came and went, but Alex noticed she was the only one who returned daily. Thorne began to single her out, speaking to her directly during group sessions.

"Alexandra understands," he would say, gesturing toward her. "She has begun to shed the illusions that bind her. The rest of you cling still to your stories of victimhood."

The praise felt like sunlight after months of winter, warming places inside her that had gone cold and numb. But it came with a price she was only beginning to understand.

He listened intently to her confessions, her fears about the divorce, her guilt over ignoring Anya, her terror that she was fundamentally unlovable. Yet he always turned her pain back upon her like a mirror, showing her twisted reflections of herself.

"Your pain," he murmured one night, leaning closer so she could smell the mint on his breath, "is proof of your resistance. You cling to wounds like a child clutching broken toys, nursing them, feeding them, making them into shrines to your own victimhood." His words cut deep, but his voice remained gentle, almost loving. "Can you not see how pathetic it is? How small?"

Tears welled in her eyes—part hurt, part shame at being seen so clearly. But then his hand brushed hers lightly, almost tenderly, and the touch sent warmth racing through her nervous system.

"I speak sharply because you are ready," he said, his voice dropping to barely above a whisper. "Others I leave in their illusions because they are too weak for truth. But you..." His fingers traced along her knuckles. "You have the strength to be carved into something magnificent."

Shame and gratitude collided inside her chest. *He sees me as strong enough for the hard truths.* The pain of his words transformed into something else—pride, even. She was special. She was chosen. She was ready for what others couldn't handle.

Her phone buzzed constantly with Anya's concern, but the messages felt like intrusions now, interruptions to the important work she was doing. "Alex, I'm worried about you. You missed lunch again. Please call me." "I saw your landlord at the grocery store. He said you're behind on rent. What's going on?" "Alex, please. Just let me know you're okay."

She silenced the phone, telling herself she was protecting Anya from the darkness of her transformation. Her sister wouldn't understand the necessity of stripping away everything false, everything comfortable, everything that kept her trapped in patterns of suffering.

Therapy sessions went unattended. Dr. Anderson had been helping her process the divorce, but now his careful questions felt invasive, his techniques shallow compared to Thorne's penetrating insights. Why waste time talking about her feelings when she could be transcending them entirely?

Donations slipped out of her bank account with increasing frequency. First twenty dollars here and there, then fifty, then hundreds. Thorne called them "offerings to the fire that will burn away your smallness."

"Energy must be exchanged," he explained during one of their private sessions. "Nothing sacred comes without sacrifice. Your money is just condensed life force—time and labor made manifest. When you offer it freely, you offer pieces of your old self to be consumed."

Each payment brought a rush of purpose, a feeling that she was finally doing something meaningful with her resources instead of wasting them on rent and groceries and other mundane necessities. Each payment also brought a reprieve from the gnawing suspicion that she was somehow unworthy of his attention.

But the more she gave, the more he seemed to expect. And the more he expected, the more she felt compelled to prove her dedication.

"I sense resistance in you still," he said one evening, his voice carrying a note of disappointment that made her stomach clench. "A holding back. A refusal to surrender completely."

"I'm trying," she whispered, though she wasn't sure what exactly she was supposed to surrender.

"Trying is the ego's way of maintaining control," he replied, settling back against his cushions. "Either you trust the process, or you don't. Either you believe I can guide you to enlightenment, or you waste both our time with half-measures."

The threat was subtle but unmistakable. She could feel his attention beginning to withdraw, could sense him losing interest in her spiritual development. Panic fluttered in her chest at the thought of being abandoned here, left to find her way alone through the maze of her own dysfunction.

"What do you need from me?" she asked, hearing the desperation in her own voice.

His smile returned, warm and approving. "Everything, Alexandra. Nothing less than everything."

***

Three weeks later, he leaned closer during one of their evening sessions, eyes glowing in the lantern light like a predator's in the darkness.

"The tent is for beginners," he said, his voice taking on a new quality—intimate, conspiratorial. "Children playing at spirituality, dabbling in wisdom they're not ready to receive. But you..." His hand found her cheek, thumb tracing along her jawline. "The true work unfolds elsewhere. In the Enlightened Enclave."

The compound sprawled beyond the carnival's edge like a hidden village, tucked into a valley where the outside world couldn't intrude. It was larger than she'd expected—dozens of structures woven together with paths lit by lanterns that kept the entire place in perpetual twilight. Small tents clustered around fire pits where people gathered in quiet circles. Meditation halls stood open to the night air. Gardens grew in precise geometric patterns that seemed to pulse with their own internal rhythm.

Disciples moved between the buildings with practiced reverence, their movements fluid and synchronized like dancers who'd rehearsed the same choreography for years. Their smiles were euphoric, radiant, but something about the uniformity of their expressions made Alex's skin crawl. They all looked *happy* in exactly the same way.

The love-bombing began immediately. A young man with kind eyes and calloused hands embraced her the moment she stepped from Thorne's vehicle.

"Welcome home, sister," Diego said, his voice thick with emotion. "You are safe here. You are loved here. Everything you've been searching for is here." His hug lasted longer than was comfortable, but Alex forced herself to accept it. This was what community felt like, she told herself. This was what she'd been missing.

A woman with prematurely gray hair and paint-stained fingers took Alex's other hand. "I'm Miriam," she said, eyes bright with unshed tears. "When I first arrived, I was broken, empty, lost. But Master Thorne saw the light within me and helped me remember who I truly am." She squeezed Alex's fingers. "I've been waiting for you. We all have."

How could they have been waiting for her? She'd only decided to come three days ago. But the warmth of their welcome, the immediate sense of belonging, felt like cool water on burnt skin. After months of isolation, of Anya's worried frowns and John's cold departure and therapists who asked invasive questions, being surrounded by people who simply accepted her felt like coming home.

A younger man bounced on his heels nearby, vibrating with barely contained excitement. "I'm Ravi," he said, his grin wide and unguarded. "I've only been here two months, but already I feel reborn. Master Thorne has shown me truths about myself I never dreamed possible. You're going to love it here, Alex. You're going to become who you were always meant to be."

The enthusiasm was infectious, but there was something manic about it that made Alex step back slightly. Ravi's pupils were dilated despite the dim lighting, and his hands trembled with what she initially took for excitement but now seemed more like nervous energy.

Presiding over it all from a raised platform was Master Thorne himself, but here he seemed different—more commanding, more regal. His stardust robes had been replaced by simple white linen that somehow made him appear more godlike rather than less. His calm never cracked, his voice never rose above a conversational tone, but every word carried the weight of absolute authority.

"You are not here to add to your life," he said, addressing the gathered disciples as Alex found her place among them on the ground. "You are here to burn it away. To strip away every false identity, every limiting belief, every comfortable lie you've been telling yourself about who you are and what you're capable of becoming."

His gaze found Alex in the crowd and held her there. "Some of you still cling to the outside world. You check your phones in secret, you long for the approval of people who do not understand your transformation, you measure your progress by the standards of a society that worships mediocrity." His voice remained gentle, but the words felt like accusations. "This attachment to the past is what keeps you trapped in patterns of suffering."

Alex felt her phone buzzing in her pocket—Anya again, probably—and shame flooded through her. He was right. She was still clinging, still divided in her commitment.

"The path requires everything," Thorne continued, his voice taking on a hypnotic rhythm that seemed to bypass her conscious mind and speak directly to something deeper. "Not most things. Not the things you can spare. Everything. Only in complete surrender can you discover what lies beyond the small, frightened ego you mistake for yourself."

***

Days unfolded with ritual precision that gradually eroded her sense of individual will. Dawn meditations began at 4:30 AM and lasted until sunrise, three hours of sitting in perfect stillness while Thorne's recorded voice guided them through visualizations designed to dissolve the boundaries of the self. By the end of the first week, Alex's legs had gone numb, her back ached constantly, and she'd begun to experience dissociative episodes where she couldn't tell if the thoughts in her head were her own or echoes of Thorne's hypnotic suggestions.

"The body protests because the ego protests," Thorne explained when she mentioned the physical discomfort. "Pain is just sensation. Suffering is the story you tell yourself about sensation. Learn to witness both without attachment, and you will discover freedom beyond anything you've ever imagined."

Hours of labor followed meditation—tending the gardens, building new structures, preparing meals for the community. But the work was never explained as simple maintenance. It was "sacred service," a form of moving meditation that purified the spirit through selfless action. Alex found herself scrubbing floors until her knuckles bled, telling herself it was devotional practice rather than exploitation.

The labor was exhausting, but worse was the way it eliminated any time for reflection or privacy. From dawn meditation to evening discourse, every moment was scheduled, every activity monitored. Even bathroom breaks were timed and tracked. Alex began to lose track of her own thoughts, her own desires, her own boundaries.

Food was rationed and carefully controlled. Breakfast consisted of thin porridge with minimal protein. Lunch was vegetables and small portions of brown rice. Dinner was often just broth and bread. Thorne explained this as purification—the body needed to be cleansed of toxins and attachments before it could become a proper vessel for enlightenment.

"Hunger is an illusion," he would say during the evening discourses, his own plate notably fuller than anyone else's. "The body believes it needs constant feeding, but this is conditioning from a culture of excess. True nourishment comes from the spirit, not from food."

But Alex noticed that while the disciples grew thinner and more hollow-eyed, Thorne himself maintained his robust appearance. His skin glowed with health, his movements remained strong and graceful. When she mentioned this observation to Miriam, the older woman's face darkened with something that looked like fear.

"Master's body is different from ours," Miriam said quickly, glancing around to make sure they weren't overheard. "He has achieved a level of spiritual development that allows him to transmute energy directly. What appears to be physical indulgence is actually a form of service—he takes on the burdens of our purification process so we don't have to."

The explanation felt hollow, but Alex found herself accepting it anyway. The alternative—that Thorne was simply taking advantage of their labor and sacrifice—was too threatening to her fragile sense of purpose to contemplate seriously.

In the evenings, after exhausting days of work and minimal food, Thorne held court in the main hall. These discourses were the highlight of each day, the moments when all the suffering and deprivation seemed worthwhile. His words dripped with paradox and profundity, weaving together fragments of Eastern philosophy, quantum physics, and mystical Christianity into a tapestry of meaning that felt revolutionary.

"Family loves you into chains," he would say, pacing slowly before his captive audience. "They claim to want your happiness, but what they really want is your compliance. They want you to remain small, manageable, predictable. True love—divine love— demands that you transcend these limiting relationships."

His tone was always calm, deliberate, as hypnotic as a snake charmer's flute. He never thundered or raged; he simply stated his truths as though describing the laws of gravity or the passage of seasons. That calmness made the words harder to resist, harder to question. This wasn't emotional manipulation—this was cosmic revelation.

"Friends praise your weakness because your strength threatens them," he continued, his gaze sweeping across the assembled disciples. "They encourage you to remain trapped in patterns of mediocrity because your transformation makes their own stagnation unbearable. Only by cutting away these energy drains can you ascend to your true potential."

Alex felt her phone gathering dust in her bag, Anya's messages piling unanswered like accusations. Each ignored call felt like proof of her spiritual growth, evidence that she was finally strong enough to prioritize her own development over others' neediness. *If I withhold, if I maintain these boundaries,* she told herself, *I am still clinging to old patterns. I have to trust the process.*

But late at night, lying on her thin mattress in the dormitory she shared with six other women, doubt crept in like smoke through cracks in a wall. The other disciples slept so deeply they seemed almost comatose, their breathing shallow and irregular. Sometimes Alex wondered if something was being added to their food or drink, some herb or chemical that kept them compliant and drowsy. But questioning the community's practices was discouraged as "ego resistance," and she'd learned to bury such thoughts before they could take root.

***

As weeks passed, Alex's role within the community began to shift. Her background in graphic design made her valuable for creating promotional materials, and Thorne began singling her out for special projects.

"Your artistic gifts are not accidents," he told her during one of their private sessions in his quarters—a spacious tent decorated with antiques and artifacts that must have cost more than most people's cars. "The divine flows through you in ways that can serve the greater work. But first, you must learn to channel that creativity toward sacred purposes rather than ego gratification."

Her art became propaganda. She designed banners declaring *The Veil Lifts For Those Who Surrender.* She created recruitment flyers with Thorne's image surrounded by geometric patterns that seemed to pulse with hypnotic energy. She illustrated books of his teachings, each page a work of devotional art that transformed his words into yantras.

The disciples praised her work with an enthusiasm that felt both wonderful and unsettling. "You channel his vision so perfectly," Miriam said, clasping her paint-stained fingers. "It's like you've become a direct conduit for his wisdom."

For fleeting moments, Alex believed it. Maybe she did matter here in ways she'd never mattered anywhere else. Maybe her failed marriage and abandoned friendships had been necessary sacrifices to prepare her for this higher purpose. Maybe Anya's concerned texts were just evidence of her sister's spiritual immaturity, her inability to understand the transformation Alex was undergoing.

But late at night, staring at her own lines and colors arranged in service to Thorne's messaging, she wondered: *Am I growing—or dissolving? Are they one and the same?*

The question felt dangerous, so she pushed it away and focused instead on perfecting the next illustration—Thorne's face emerging from lotus petals, his eyes seeming to follow the viewer with benevolent authority.

**

The dissonance deepened as Alex became more integrated into the community's inner workings. She noticed things that didn't align with Thorne's teachings about equality and shared sacrifice. His quarters were luxurious while the disciples slept on thin mattresses in overcrowded dormitories. His meals were elaborate affairs prepared by a rotating staff of female disciples while the rest of the community subsisted on rationed portions. He wore expensive jewelry—rings and bracelets that caught the light during his evening discourses—while preaching about the spiritual dangers of material attachment.

When she mentioned these observations to other disciples, their responses were always the same: deflection, rationalization, or gentle correction about her failure to understand the deeper mysteries at work.

"Master's comfort serves the community," Diego explained when Alex asked about the obvious disparity. "If his body is not properly nourished, if his mind is distracted by physical concerns, how can he channel the teachings we need? His well-being is our well-being."

But Alex noticed that Diego's own ribs were becoming visible through his work shirt, and dark circles shadowed his once-kind eyes. The cognitive dissonance created a constant low-level anxiety that she tried to medicate through more intensive spiritual practice. If she could just surrender more completely, she told herself, these troubling thoughts would dissolve into the peace she saw on other disciples' faces.

The breaking point began with Ravi. The young man's manic enthusiasm had gradually transformed into something darker—a kind of desperate clinging that made others avoid him during community gatherings. He'd started asking questions during the evening discourses, tentative inquiries that suggested his faith was beginning to crack.

89

"Master, forgive my ignorance," he said one night, his voice measured and careful, "but why must our bodies be pushed beyond their limits? I understand that suffering can be a teacher, but some of the newer disciples are becoming ill from exhaustion. Is suffering truly the only path to enlightenment?"

The question hung in the air like smoke from a snuffed candle. Alex felt her heart rate spike, partly from fear of how Thorne would respond and partly from relief that someone had finally voiced what many of them were thinking.

Thorne's response was vintage manipulation wrapped in spiritual authority. His smile never wavered, his voice remained calm and loving, but Alex could see something predatory gleaming behind his eyes.

"The body protests because the ego protests," he said, settling back against his cushions with studied grace. "Fatigue is the ego's last disguise, its final attempt to maintain control over the soul's evolution. When you feel your strength failing, when you want to rest or eat or comfort yourself, that is not your body speaking— that is fear. That is resistance. That is the small, frightened child within you trying to keep you trapped in patterns of mediocrity."

He leaned forward slightly, his gaze pinning Ravi in place like a butterfly on display. "Tell me, my child, would you choose the comfort of a dream, or the fire of truth? Would you remain asleep in pleasant illusions, or wake up to the magnificent suffering that transforms caterpillars into butterflies?"

Ravi bowed his head, trembling, silenced by the gentle force of Thorne's certainty. The circle of disciples murmured their assent, nodding along with the master's wisdom. Alex found herself nodding too, though her heart was racing with something that felt like terror. It sounded holy, didn't it? The metaphor was beautiful, the logic seemed sound. But underneath the lyrical phrasing, she sensed something wrong—a crack in the foundation that threatened to bring down everything she'd built her new identity around.

She forced herself to appear convinced, shame boiling under her skin at her own cowardice. Why couldn't she simply trust the process? Why did doubt keep creeping in like poison through the cracks of her surrender?

After the discourse ended and the disciples dispersed to their quarters, Alex lingered in the shadows near the main hall. She told herself she was just clearing her mind before sleep, but part of her was hoping to overhear something that would either confirm or dispel her growing suspicions.

What she heard instead was worse than she'd imagined.

Voices carried from Thorne's quarters—his own distinctive cadence mixed with Diego's more tentative tones. Alex crept closer, her heart hammering against her ribs as she strained to listen.

"Redirect the offerings to the private account," Thorne was saying, his voice carrying none of the cosmic gravitas it held during public teachings. Here, in what he believed to be privacy, he sounded like any other person conducting business. "The renovation budget, the food allowances, the community expenses—funnel it through the shell company. The vessel must be nourished, or it cannot hold the light."

"But Master," Diego's voice was barely audible, strained with something that might have been desperation, "some of the disciples are asking questions about the financial arrangements. They're wondering why their donations aren't being used for community improvements."

Thorne's laugh was soft but chilling, devoid of the warmth he displayed during public appearances. "Let them wonder. Curiosity about mundane matters is just another form of resistance. The ones who question are the ones who aren't ready for the deeper teachings anyway."

There was a pause, then Thorne's voice continued with casual cruelty that made Alex's stomach turn. "If they're not satisfied with the accommodations, they're free to leave. We're not running a resort here—we're facilitating spiritual evolution. Comfort is the enemy of growth."

Alex froze in the shadows, ice water flooding her veins. The man speaking bore no resemblance to the enlightened master who held court each evening. This voice belonged to someone who saw his followers not as spiritual seekers but as resources to be managed and exploited.

She tried to rationalize what she'd heard. Maybe there were layers of meaning she wasn't sophisticated enough to understand. Maybe the financial arrangements served purposes beyond her current level of spiritual development. But the casual dismissal in Thorne's tone, the complete absence of compassion for his followers' suffering, felt like a knife between her shoulder blades.

We starve while he feasts, she thought, the realization hitting her like a physical blow. We break our bodies in service while he accumulates comfort. This isn't about spiritual growth—this is about power.

But even as the thought formed, another voice in her head—trained by months of conditioning—whispered that her doubt was just ego resistance, just another test of her commitment to the path. The internal war between her growing awareness and her desperate need to believe left her feeling fractured, as though she were splitting into multiple people who couldn't agree on what was real.

***

The situation with Ravi deteriorated rapidly after that night. His questions became more frequent and more pointed, his desperate enthusiasm curdling into something that looked like panic. Alex could see herself reflected in his growing desperation—the same need to make sense of the contradictions, the same terror at the possibility that everything they'd sacrificed had been for nothing.

During work assignments, Ravi began muttering to himself, fragments of doubt and confusion that he tried to voice quietly enough that the supervisors wouldn't hear. "Why do we build his comfort while we sleep on floors? Why does he eat meat while we're told protein corrupts the spirit? Why are we forbidden from contacting family when he has visitors from outside every week?"

Alex wanted to respond, wanted to acknowledge that she shared his concerns, but the community had trained her well. Questioning another disciple's spiritual progress was discouraged. Expressing doubt was considered a form of psychic pollution that could infect others. The safest response was to maintain loving silence and trust that Thorne would address any necessary corrections.

But Ravi's breakdown was becoming impossible to ignore. He'd lost significant weight, his hands shook constantly, and dark circles shadowed his eyes. During meditation sessions, he would rock back and forth, lips moving in silent prayer or argument. Other disciples began avoiding him, their expressions mixing pity with fear—fear that his spiritual crisis might be contagious.

The confrontation came during an evening discourse three days later. Thorne was expounding on the necessity of absolute trust in divine authority when Ravi suddenly stood up in the middle of the circle.

"Why must we starve while you dine on delicacies?" he asked, his voice cracking with exhaustion and desperation. "Why must we sleep on floors while you rest in luxury? If we're all equal on this path, why are we treated like servants while you live like a king?"

The silence that followed felt like the moment before lightning strikes. Alex could feel the collective intake of breath from the assembled disciples, the shock and horror at such direct challenge to their master's authority. Some of them looked physically ill, as though Ravi had committed an act of violence rather than asked reasonable questions.

Thorne's response was masterful in its calculated cruelty. For a long moment, he simply regarded Ravi with the patient expression of a parent dealing with a troubled child. When he finally spoke, his voice carried disappointed sadness rather than anger—somehow making his rejection more devastating than rage would have been.

"Your doubt poisons this sacred circle," he said, his tone heavy with regret. "You bring the energy of suspicion and resentment into a space dedicated to love and growth. You corrupt the very air we breathe with your toxic questions."

He stood slowly, gracefully, his movements deliberate and hypnotic. "You are filth in the river of our shared consciousness. You are pollution in the temple of our community. You have become a wound that threatens to infect the healthy tissue around it."

Ravi began to shake, his face crumpling as though he were being physically struck. The other disciples watched in fascination and horror, their expressions mixing relief that they weren't the target with terror that they might be next.

"Kneel," Thorne commanded, his voice taking on the quality of absolute authority that Alex had heard him use during her early sessions. "Beg forgiveness from this community you have violated with your ego-driven accusations. Purge yourself of this poison, or be cast into the abyss of your own spiritual poverty."

What happened next would haunt Alex for years afterward. Ravi collapsed to his knees as though invisible hands had forced him down. Tears streamed down his face as he began to beg—not just for forgiveness, but for the chance to remain in the community, to continue serving, to prove his devotion despite his momentary weakness.

"Please, Master," he sobbed, his words barely intelligible. "Please don't abandon me. I'm sorry, I'm so sorry. The doubt isn't real, it's just my ego trying to destroy everything beautiful in my life. Please let me stay. Please help me be worthy of your teachings."

The disciples bowed their heads, paralyzed by the display of absolute power. Some of them were crying too—whether from empathy for Ravi or relief at their own escape from judgment, Alex couldn't tell. The energy in the room felt thick and suffocating, charged with a combination of fear, shame, and terrible fascination.

And through it all, Thorne stood over Ravi's broken form with an expression of benevolent authority, but Alex caught something else in his eyes—a fleeting moment when his mask slipped, revealing not enlightened compassion but the satisfied gleam of a predator savoring its dominance over wounded prey.

This is not awakening, Alex realized with crystalline clarity. *This is devouring.*

The recognition struck her like a thunderclap in the silence, forcing her to clutch the cushion to steady herself against the invisible force. Heat surged through her veins in a furious rush, as if her very skin might burst into flame from the intensity. Her vision blurred under the pressure of unshed tears, pent-up and straining like a river against a fracturing dam. Meanwhile, her mind detonated—expanding wildly, forging connections between every overlooked fragment from her months with Thorne. Everything she'd witnessed—the financial exploitation, the food rationing, the isolation from outside contacts, the endless labor disguised as spiritual service—suddenly reconfigured itself into a pattern she could finally see clearly.

Thorne wasn't a spiritual master guiding seekers toward enlightenment. He was a predator who had learned to speak the language of transcendence while feeding on the vulnerabilities of people desperate for meaning, healing, and belonging. The community wasn't a spiritual family—it was a carefully constructed web designed to trap people exactly like her, people whose wounds and longings made them perfect prey.

But even as the truth crystallized in her mind, another part of her resisted. The part that had been lovingly shaped by months of conditioning whispered that this was just another test, another opportunity to demonstrate her faith in the face of apparent contradictions. Maybe Ravi's humiliation was necessary for his spiritual growth. Maybe her doubt was exactly the kind of ego resistance Thorne had warned her about from the beginning.

The internal war left her feeling nauseated and dizzy. She wanted to stand up, to defend Ravi, to demand answers about the contradictions she'd observed. But the weight of the community's expectation, the fear of becoming the next target of Thorne's disappointed correction, kept her frozen in place.

After what felt like hours but was probably only minutes, Thorne finally granted Ravi forgiveness with the magnanimous grace of a king pardoning a traitor. The young man was allowed to remain in the community, but his status had clearly shifted. Other disciples avoided him, treating him like someone recovering from a contagious disease. His work assignments became more menial, his access to private teachings was revoked, and he was required to undergo daily "purification sessions" with Thorne to cleanse himself of his spiritual toxicity.

Alex watched Ravi's systematic degradation with a mixture of pity and terror. The bright-eyed young man who had welcomed her with such enthusiasm was being methodically broken down, rebuilt as a cautionary tale for anyone else who might consider questioning the master's wisdom.

***

Her own special status within the community became both a blessing and a curse. Thorne continued to single her out for private instruction and artistic projects, but Alex now noticed the predatory calculation behind his attention. She was valuable to him—not as a student, but as a tool. Her design skills served his recruitment efforts, her spiritual insights (carefully shaped by his guidance) provided testimonials for his teachings, and her gradual transformation from broken divorce to devoted disciple offered proof of his power to potential followers.

During their private sessions, Thorne's behavior became increasingly inappropriate in ways that were subtle enough to leave her questioning her own perceptions. His hands would linger on her shoulders during "energy work." His compliments about her spiritual progress would be mixed with comments about her physical appearance. He would position himself closer to her than necessary during instruction, close enough that she could smell the expensive cologne he wore despite preaching about detachment from material luxuries.

"Your energy is opening beautifully," he said during one session, his fingers tracing along her spine under the guise of adjusting her meditation posture. "I can feel the sacred feminine awakening within you. It's a powerful force that requires careful guidance to channel properly."

Alex's skin crawled, but she forced herself to remain still. This was spiritual instruction, she told herself. Sacred touch was different from ordinary physical contact. If she felt uncomfortable, that was just her ego creating resistance to a higher form of healing.

But when his hands moved to her ribcage, ostensibly checking her breathing but lingering in ways that felt invasive, she couldn't suppress a small flinch.

"Still some armor here," Thorne murmured, his voice taking on the hypnotic quality she'd come to associate with his deeper teachings. "The heart chakra is protected by walls built from past trauma. Your husband's betrayal created barriers that prevent you from receiving divine love. We'll need to work on dissolving those defenses."

His touch became more deliberate, more intimate, justified through spiritual language that made it difficult to object without seeming spiritually immature. Alex found herself dissociating during these sessions, floating above her body while Thorne's hands explored territories that had nothing to do with chakras or energy work.

Afterward, she would feel contaminated and confused, unable to reconcile what had happened with the spiritual framework that was supposed to make sense of her experience. When she tried to process these feelings with other disciples, their responses were invariably supportive of Thorne's methods.

"Master's healing work operates on levels we don't always understand," Miriam explained when Alex tentatively described her discomfort. "He can see blockages and traumas that we're not even conscious of. Sometimes the healing process involves experiencing touch in new ways, breaking down the barriers that keep us separated from divine love."

But Alex noticed that Miriam's eyes didn't meet hers during this explanation, and her voice carried the flat quality of someone reciting memorized responses rather than expressing genuine belief.

***

The sexual exploitation within the community became impossible to ignore as Alex gained deeper access to the inner workings of the group. Rumors circulated like incense smoke— whispered conversations about "sacred unions" and "tantric initiations" that were reserved for the most spiritually advanced disciples.

Thorne had begun selecting certain women for special overnight sessions, framing these encounters as profound spiritual experiences rather than what they clearly were. The chosen disciples would return from his quarters with brittle smiles and hollow eyes, their responses to questions carefully scripted to emphasize the transcendent nature of their experiences.

"It's not what people on the outside would understand," Ingrid, a newer recruit with flowing auburn hair, explained when Alex asked about her overnight instruction. "Master works with sacred sexuality to help us transcend the ego's attachment to the body. It's a form of worship that dissolves the boundaries between self and divine."

But Ingrid's hands shook as she spoke, and Alex caught her vomiting in the communal bathroom later that same morning. When their eyes met, Ingrid's expression flickered between shame and desperate need for validation before settling into the practiced serenity all disciples were expected to maintain.

Alex's own sessions with Thorne were escalating in ways that terrified her. His "energy work" had progressed to requiring partial nudity, justified through elaborate explanations about the need to access certain meridian points without clothing interference. His comments about her spiritual development had become increasingly sexualized, framed in language about divine feminine energy and sacred receptivity.

"You're ready for the deeper teachings," he told her during their latest session, his hands resting possessively on her bare shoulders. "The ultimate mysteries can only be transmitted through direct energetic exchange. Most people aren't spiritually developed enough to handle that level of intimacy with the divine, but you..." His fingers traced along her collarbone. "You have the strength to receive what I have to offer."

The implication was clear, and Alex felt panic rising in her chest like floodwater. But when she tried to express hesitation, Thorne's response was swift and calculated.

"I sense fear," he said, his voice taking on that disappointed tone that had become one of her greatest dreads. "The wounded feminine within you is still protecting itself from the very healing it needs most. This resistance is what keeps you trapped in patterns of loneliness and betrayal."

He withdrew his hands, and Alex immediately felt the absence of his attention like a physical chill. "Perhaps you're not ready after all," he continued, settling back against his cushions with an air of regretful acceptance. "The advanced teachings require complete trust, absolute surrender. If you're still clinging to ordinary concepts of propriety, if you're still letting your traumatized psyche dictate your spiritual choices, then we should return to the basic practices until you've developed greater faith."

The threat of abandonment sent Alex into a spiral of desperate need to prove her worthiness. The months of conditioning had taught her that Thorne's approval was the only thing standing between her and the abyss of meaninglessness she'd fallen into after her divorce. Without his guidance, without her place in this community, she would have nothing—no purpose, no identity, no protection from the crushing emptiness that had driven her to the spiritual carnival in the first place.

"No, please," she heard herself saying, hating the pleading tone in her voice but unable to stop it. "I want to learn. I want to receive the deeper teachings. The fear isn't real—it's just conditioning from the past. I trust you completely."

Thorne's smile returned, warm and approving, and Alex felt the familiar flood of relief and gratitude that had become her drug of choice. She was special again. She was chosen. She was worthy of his attention and guidance.

But underneath the artificial euphoria, a small voice screamed warnings that she couldn't afford to hear.

***

The breaking point came not through gradual realization but through a moment of stark clarity that cut through months of conditioning like lightning through fog. It happened during a midnight ritual that Thorne had framed as a special ceremony for the most advanced disciples—Alex, Ingrid, Miriam, and two other women who had been selected for what he called "the ultimate initiation."

The ritual began in the main hall, with hours of chanting designed to induce altered states of consciousness. The repetitive sounds, combined with the food deprivation and sleep exhaustion that had become Alex's normal state, created a dissociative trance that made everything feel dreamlike and unreal.

The selected disciples were led to Thorne's private quarters, where the ceremony was supposed to reach its climax. The room had been transformed with candles, incense, and silk draping that created an atmosphere of sacred sexuality. Cushions were arranged in patterns that suggested the women were meant to serve as offerings in some elaborate ritual of transcendence.

But as the ceremony progressed, as Thorne's instructions became more explicitly sexual and the other women began to comply with mechanical obedience, Alex experienced a moment of perfect clarity that shattered all her carefully constructed rationalizations.

She saw Ingrid's face in the candlelight—not transcendent, not spiritually elevated, but empty and dissociated, going through motions that had nothing to do with divine love and everything to do with survival. She saw Miriam trembling with what wasn't ecstasy but terror, her eyes focused on some point beyond the ceiling as though she were trying to escape her own body. She saw the other women moving with the practiced efficiency of people who had learned that compliance was the only path to safety.

And in that moment, Alex finally understood what she was looking at. This wasn't sacred sexuality or divine union or any of the other spiritual concepts Thorne had used to frame his exploitation. This was systematic abuse, dressed up in mystical language and justified through elaborate theological constructions that made resistance feel like spiritual failure.

We are not disciples, she realized with crystalline clarity. *We are victims.*

The recognition was so powerful, so complete, that it cut through every layer of conditioning and manipulation Thorne had built around her mind. She saw him not as an enlightened master but as a predator who had learned to weaponize people's deepest spiritual longings against them. She saw the community not as a spiritual family but as a web designed to trap and exploit the vulnerable.

Most importantly, she saw herself—not as a broken woman who needed Thorne's guidance to become whole, but as someone whose very wounds had been turned into chains.

With movements that felt mechanical, disconnected from conscious decision, Alex stood up and walked toward the door. Thorne's voice followed her, sharp with command despite its maintained veneer of spiritual authority.

"Alexandra, you are allowing fear to rob you of the most profound gift you will ever receive. This resistance is the final test of your ego before it dissolves into divine love. If you leave now, you abandon not just this ceremony but your entire spiritual evolution."

She paused at the threshold, part of her still trapped by months of conditioning that insisted his words carried ultimate truth. But then she heard something else—Ingrid's quiet sob, barely audible beneath Thorne's practiced manipulation. The sound cut through her paralysis like a blade.

"I can't," Alex whispered, not turning around. "This isn't right. This isn't love. This isn't anything but harm dressed up in pretty words."

She stepped outside into air that felt shockingly clean after the suffocating atmosphere of Thorne's quarters. Behind her, she heard his voice shift—the spiritual authority dropping away to reveal something cold and calculating underneath.

"You're making a terrible mistake," he said, no longer bothering with mystical rhetoric. "You have no idea how to survive without this community, without my guidance. You'll crawl back within a week, begging to be readmitted. And when you do, you'll find that mercy has limits."

The threat was clear, but for the first time in months, Alex felt something stronger than fear coursing through her system. It was anger—clean, righteous anger at being manipulated, exploited, and nearly destroyed by someone who had positioned himself as her savior.

She didn't respond to his words. Instead, she walked away from his quarters and toward the edge of the compound, each step loosening the psychological chains that had bound her for so long.

**

Leaving the physical space proved easier than leaving the mental conditioning. As Alex made her way through the compound's darkened pathways, disciples emerged from their quarters to watch her go. Some looked confused, others appeared frightened, but none tried to stop her. They had been trained too well to interfere with what their master had decided.

Only Ravi appeared from the shadows as she reached the compound's entrance. The young man who had once bubbled with enthusiasm was now gaunt and hollow-eyed, his spirit broken by weeks of systematic punishment for his earlier questions.

"You're really leaving?" he asked, his voice barely above a whisper.

"Yes," Alex replied, though the word felt strange in her mouth after months of being trained to suppress her own will.

"Take me with you," Ravi begged, grabbing her arm with desperate fingers. "Please. I can't stay here anymore, but I don't know how to leave alone. I'm afraid of what he'll do if I try to go by myself."

Alex looked at his haunted face and saw her own terror reflected back at her. But she also saw something else—the same spark of rebellion that had driven her own escape, the same refusal to be completely consumed that had saved her from total destruction.

"Come on," she said, extending her hand. "We'll figure it out together."

They slipped away from the compound in the pre-dawn darkness, two refugees from a war most people didn't even know was being fought. The carnival grounds were nearly empty, most of the vendors and performers still asleep in their trailers and tents. The familiar chaos of the spiritual marketplace that had once seemed overwhelming now felt like a symphony of freedom compared to the suffocating control they'd left behind.

As they reached the carnival's outer limits, she heard voices in the distance—Thorne's disciples beginning their dawn meditation, their chanted surrender to his will carrying on the morning air like a funeral dirge.

Her hands trembled as she continued to walk, months of psychological conditioning warring with her desperate need to escape. Part of her still insisted that leaving was spiritual failure, that she was abandoning her only chance for true growth and meaning. But a stronger part—the part that had finally remembered her own voice—knew that staying would mean losing herself entirely.

As they journeyed away from the compound, away from the carnival, away from the elaborate web of manipulation that had nearly consumed her, Alex felt something she hadn't experienced in months: the terrifying, exhilarating sensation of making her own choices.

The path ahead was uncertain, filled with the difficult work of recovery and rebuilding. But it was her path now, chosen by her own will rather than dictated by someone else's hunger for control.

In her pocket, her phone buzzed with accumulated messages— Anya's voice reaching across months of enforced silence like a lifeline thrown to someone drowning. Alex took a seat on the side of the path, her fingers shaking as she dialed her sister's number.

The phone rang once. Twice.

"Alex?" Anya's voice cracked with fear and relief and love so pure it brought tears to Alex's eyes.

"It's me," she whispered, her voice hoarse from months of chanting surrender to someone else's will. "I want to come home."

The conversation that followed would be the first of many difficult ones, part of a long journey back to herself that would require professional help, patient love from people who hadn't tried to exploit her vulnerabilities, and the slow, painful work of learning to trust her own judgment again.

But as she sat on that long empty path with Ravi beside her—both of them squinting at the dawn like creatures emerging from a cave—Alex felt something she had almost forgotten existed: hope.

The light she had been seeking wasn't hidden in lanterns or silk draping or the hypnotic gaze of a false master. It had been inside her all along, waiting patiently through months of psychological torture for her to remember that freedom, terrifying and uncertain as it might be, was always preferable to the gilded cage of someone else's control.

The guru's shadow had nearly consumed her, but in the end, her own inner light had proven stronger than his manufactured darkness. That light—fragile but unbreakable, wounded but still burning—would guide her home.

Alex's journey illuminates the razor's edge between sacred surrender and spiritual enslavement. Her experience reveals what the circus conceals: that the human soul is inherently communal, desperately seeking something greater than the isolation of modern individualism. This seeking is not weakness—it is the deepest expression of our nature as meaning-making beings. We are creatures who require narrative, belonging, purpose, transcendence. The tragedy is not that we seek these things, but that predators have learned to manufacture synthetic versions that poison the very needs they claim to fulfill.

The word "cult" itself has become a scarlet letter in our cultural vocabulary, yet it originally meant nothing more sinister than "cultivation"—the tending of something sacred, the careful nurturing of growth. Like fire, this cultivation can warm a home or consume a forest. The difference lies not in the flame itself, but in who tends it and toward what end.

Yet we might ask ourselves: what distinguishes the cultivation we label "cult" from the cultivation we call normal? Consider the millions who gather weekly in structures crowned with spires, following ancient texts and surrendering portions of their income to collective purposes. Consider those who pledge allegiance to flags, who organize their entire existence around corporate cultures, who dedicate themselves to causes larger than individual desire. These too are forms of cultivation—systems of shared meaning that shape identity and behavior through group dynamics and collective ritual. We do not name them cults because their tentacles have grown so vast, so normalized, that we mistake the familiar weight of their influence for freedom itself.

In the circus of spirituality, we encounter two breeds of cultivator. The authentic teacher offers themselves as compost for your growth, disappearing into your flourishing rather than feeding upon it. They point toward your own inner authority with the patience of a gardener who knows that forced blooming creates only the illusion of flowers. True cultivation plants seeds in soil that remains your own.

But in the shadow tents, we find the farmers of human desperation—those who have studied the seasons of vulnerability and learned to plant dependency where liberation was promised. They harvest not vegetables but agency itself, not fruit but the very capacity for independent thought. Their gardens produce not nourishment but hunger—endless, gnawing hunger that only they can temporarily satisfy.

The dark triad—narcissism, Machiavellianism, psychopathy— represents cultivation turned malignant. Where healthy spiritual communities nurture the individual within the collective, these pathological systems require the individual to be digested by it. The leader becomes not a temporary guide but a permanent necessity, not a stepping stone but a throne that must be fed with constant tribute of attention, resources, and surrendered will.

Thorne's method was not unique in its essence, only in its particular artistry. The pattern repeats across the carnival with the reliability of natural law: the identification of vulnerability, the offering of immediate relief, the gradual escalation of commitment, the systematic isolation from alternative sources of meaning, the reframing of natural resistance as spiritual deficiency, the intermittent rewards that create addiction to approval, and finally the complete replacement of the victim's internal compass with the perpetrator's desires.

What makes spiritual predation particularly insidious is its appropriation of our highest aspirations. Physical violence we can recognize, financial fraud eventually reveals itself, but psychological manipulation cloaked in transcendent language attacks our very capacity to distinguish between evolution and dissolution, between growth and erosion, between love and control. The victim becomes complicit in their own destruction, believing they are participating in their salvation.

Yet Alex's escape reveals the fault line in even the most sophisticated systems of control: the irreducible core of human consciousness that remains, like a seed beneath snow, capable of recognizing its own nature when conditions permit. No amount of conditioning can completely extinguish the inner voice that whispers the difference between authentic and artificial, between nourishment and consumption, between teachers who liberate and those who imprison.

The circus seeker must develop what we might call spiritual immunity—the ability to distinguish between groups that enhance human flourishing and those that diminish it. This discrimination requires not cynicism, which closes the heart to all possibility, but discernment, which opens it wisely.

Watch for the direction the river flows through any spiritual community. Does power move toward individual empowerment or centralized control? Are questions welcomed as sacred inquiry or punished as spiritual treason? Does the group create conditions for members to eventually outgrow their need for it, or does it foster permanent dependence? Are resources shared honestly or concentrated in leadership's hands? Is doubt met with patient dialogue or with shame and ostracism?

Most crucially: does participation increase your capacity for independent thought and authentic relationship, or does it require the progressive surrender of these capabilities? True cultivation produces students who become teachers, followers who become leaders, dependents who become sovereign. False cultivation produces only more efficient servants to the cultivator's will.

The seeker's path through the spiritual circus is ultimately a hero's journey through the landscape of their own discriminating wisdom. Each encounter—whether with charlatan or sage, predator or guide—offers data about your capacity to distinguish between what serves your highest good and what merely serves another's appetites.

Alex emerged from Thorne's shadow not because she was uniquely strong, but because she finally remembered what strength actually felt like. Underneath the conditioning, beneath the elaborate theology of her own inadequacy, the original self remained intact—wounded but not broken, confused but not destroyed, temporarily enslaved but eternally free.

This is the promise and the peril of the spiritual path: that in seeking transcendence, we might encounter both the genuine article and its most cunning imitation. The circus will always contain both real medicine and elaborate poison, sometimes in adjacent tents, sometimes in the same cup. Yet we must understand what the circus actually represents—not the spiritual path itself, but a glittering distraction from it. It is entirely human to be excited, captured, and caught up in its promises; this natural curiosity and longing deserves no criticism. But the circus operates through illusions that keep sincere seekers going in circles, mistaking movement for progress, spectacle for substance. Our task is not to judge ourselves for being drawn to its lights, but to develop the discernment that recognizes when we've wandered from the path into the sideshow—and the wisdom to find our way back to the genuine journey of awakening.

The false guru's power exists only when you doubt your own inner knowing. Trust that inner voice when it whispers that something feels wrong, and no manipulator can long deceive you —no matter how spiritually they present themselves. The teacher you seek is not in the tent ahead but in the mirror of your own deepening discernment. The freedom you crave is not found in any doctrine but in your unshakeable commitment to your own authentic unfolding.

In the end, the greatest master seeks no slaves, but only to liberate those who have enslaved themselves.

A Pocket-Sized Carnival

Picture this: you wake up, grab your phone, and within seconds you're scrolling past profound quotes from Rumi overlaid on sunset photos, influencers in ceremonial headdresses they bought on Etsy discussing indigenous wisdom, goddesses in revealing robes teaching sacred sexuality from their bedrooms, someone dancing topless in a forest while narrating chakra alignment, artists with hand drums on mountaintops summoning the divine through "light language", and astrology accounts promising portal activations and DNA upgrades—all before your feet hit the floor. Welcome to the endless digital midway of social media, where the entire spiritual carnival has been compressed into pocket-sized reality and beams its attractions directly into our consciousness every moment of the day.

In our exploration of the spiritual carnival, we've wandered through many territories—past the fortune tellers with their crystalline promises, beyond the workshop stages where weekend warriors peddle transformation, and into the darker compounds where false masters build empires from devotion. But now we come to territory that exists everywhere and nowhere simultaneously, where the metaphor becomes literal. Every spiritual seeker, teacher, and charlatan carries their own pocket-sized carnival booth, broadcasting their wares twenty-four hours a day to an audience of billions.

The numbers tell an extraordinary story that spans continents. Hashtags like #WitchTok have accumulated over 20 billion views, while #Astrology leads with 41.1 billion views on TikTok alone in the United States—but globally, TikTok's #spirituality hashtag has exploded to 48.4 billion views from 5.5 million posts, with #spiritual generating another 19.1 billion views. These aren't niche communities—they represent more engagement than many mainstream entertainment categories, creating a $376 billion global spiritual services market in 2024 that projects to reach $787.4 billion by 2035.

What we're witnessing is the largest shift in spiritual practice since the internet's inception, driven primarily by Gen Z across the globe. While American Gen Z identifies as 77% spiritual versus 68% religious, this generational transformation ripples worldwide —from Scandinavian countries where Swedish Millennials show 38% believing in afterlife with 32% believing nature has spirits, to South Korea where 53% claim no religion (the highest globally), to Asia-Pacific markets commanding 31% of the global spiritual services market worth $116.6 billion.

This digital midway operates on different rules than the physical carnival. Where once you had to choose which tent to enter, which teacher to follow, which path to walk, now you can sample them all in the space of a single scroll session. Ancient Tibetan meditation techniques flow seamlessly into Brazilian plant medicine ceremonies, which dissolve into Nordic shamanic practices, all served up as bite-sized content optimized for maximum engagement rather than genuine transformation.

The barriers between performer and audience have collapsed entirely—everyone is simultaneously the act and the spectator, the vendor and the customer, the seeker and the sought. The carnival's traditional operators have become algorithm engineers, and they've discovered something their predecessors never dreamed of: they can make the customers perform for themselves.

Every post, every share, every carefully curated glimpse of spiritual insight becomes both advertisement and product. The seekers have become the show, performing their own seeking for the entertainment and validation of other performers masquerading as seekers. From North America's 34,200 certified coaches to Western Europe's 30,800 to Asia-Pacific's estimated 20,000, spiritual influencers maintain engagement rates that exceed industry benchmarks—wellness content achieving 4.0% monthly follower growth on TikTok with 18% engagement rates for nano-influencers, while traditional business accounts struggle at 0.56%.

What we're witnessing is the complete gamification of the spiritual path. The ancient practices that once required years of disciplined study, silence, and surrender have been repackaged as content—consumable, shareable, and above all, profitable. The sacred has been democratized and commodified simultaneously, creating a marketplace where anyone can be a teacher and everyone is a student, but no one has time to actually learn anything deeply.

The cruel genius of this system lies in how it exploits the noblest human impulses. The desire for growth becomes the compulsion to share insights before they've been integrated. The longing for community becomes the addiction to likes and comments from strangers. The search for meaning becomes the pursuit of viral content. The sacred act of surrendering the ego becomes the endless performance of ego in spiritual drag.

In this digital realm, the spiritual seeker faces a new kind of predator—not the charismatic guru demanding submission to their authority, but an algorithmic system that turns them into their own oppressor. The prison bars are made not of physical isolation but of endless stimulation. The guard is not another human being but their own fragmented attention, scattered across a thousand different spiritual teachers, practices, and philosophies, never settling long enough on any one thing to allow genuine transformation to occur.

This phenomenon has created a new category of spiritual entrepreneur—the aspiring mystic who builds their entire teaching foundation on imitation and projection. These are not the established masters who skillfully employ social platforms as tools of outreach, pointing toward the deeper practices they've spent decades developing. Those seasoned teachers understand the medium's limitations and use it consciously—sharing glimpses that inspire seeking while directing sincere students toward substantial, offline work.

Instead, we see a generation of spiritual aspirants who mistake their early insights for mastery, their enthusiasm for wisdom, their online following for spiritual authority. They study the aesthetics of enlightenment—the right poses, the perfect settings, the mystical-sounding phrases—and perform these borrowed elements to build personal brands around their projected understanding of ancient knowledge.

The meditation teacher with six months of practice positions themselves alongside lineage holders with decades of training. The self-proclaimed shaman markets plant medicine ceremonies after a handful of ayahuasca experiences in Costa Rica or a transformative mushroom journey in their bedroom—suddenly qualified to guide others through realms they've barely begun to navigate themselves. The tantric goddess channels raw sexual appetite through spiritual rhetoric, promising liberation of the feminine divine while offering workshops that would make actual tantric practitioners vomit. With 122,974 certified coach practitioners globally in 2025—representing a 15% increase since 2023—credentialing has become as simple as printing business cards and claiming expertise across cultural boundaries.

These new mystics are not necessarily malicious—many genuinely believe in their offering and experience real benefit from the practices they promote. But they operate in a feedback loop where online validation confirms their self-appointed authority, where follower counts substitute for actual mastery, where the ability to create engaging content becomes confused with the ability to guide spiritual development.

The seekers themselves become collectors of spiritual trading cards—gathering mindfulness quotes, chakra diagrams, meditation techniques from dozens of teachers, manifestation hacks from countless gurus. This endless variety creates the sensation of learning and growing while actually preventing the depth of engagement necessary for real transformation. They mistake the map for the territory, the menu for the meal, the packaging for the gift.

The digital spiritual marketplace breeds its own form of materialism—one where the markers of authenticity themselves become commodities. Crystals positioned just right in the frame, perfectly curated meditation spaces, exotic retreat locations as backdrops, esoteric terminology sprinkled throughout captions, mysterious symbols as profile decorations. All become props in elaborate performances of enlightenment, teaching seekers to speak the language of awakening while remaining thoroughly asleep to their own conditioning.

Yet perhaps the most profound disruption occurs to the faculty that every contemplative tradition considers essential: sustained attention. The ability to rest in stillness, to observe without immediately reacting, to remain present with what is rather than seeking what might be—these capacities require the very quality that social media systematically undermines. While popular claims about attention spans declining to 8 seconds from 12 seconds have been thoroughly debunked by UK research from King's College London, comprehensive international meta-analysis reveals that digital technology effects depend significantly on users' characteristics, cultural context, and usage patterns rather than simple exposure.

Different cultures process attention differently—American children excel at focusing on single objects while Japanese children naturally see broader patterns and relationships. But regardless of these cultural variations, the endless scroll creates the same problem everywhere: restless seeking, constant stimulation, perpetual dissatisfaction with the present moment.

Silence—revered by every authentic tradition as the space where wisdom emerges—becomes intolerable. The gaps between activities, the spaces between thoughts, the moments when nothing exciting is happening become voids demanding immediate filling with content consumption. What emerges is a kind of spiritual attention deficit: the inability to rest long enough for genuine understanding to dawn.

But here lies an unexpected paradox. While social media fragments attention, research from multiple countries reveals that brief meditation sessions of 10-13 minutes prove more effective than traditional longer practices for modern practitioners. Studies involving 8 weeks of daily 13-minute meditation enhanced attention, working memory, and mood—a finding replicated across diverse cultural contexts. Chinese research by Tang et al. demonstrated that 7 days of 30-minute practice among undergraduates produced significant improvements in creative thinking and emotional regulation, while European research adaptations show equivalent effectiveness to original Eastern practices, suggesting cross-cultural validity for brief meditation interventions.

This raises the central question this territory demands we address: How do we reclaim the sacred in an economy that profits from its destruction? How do we distinguish between platforms as skillful tools and platforms as spiritual overlords? How do we preserve the quiet, unglamorous, un-postable work of genuine transformation in a world that only rewards what can be performed, shared, and monetized?

The revolutionary possibility lies in using these same platforms skillfully. Despite all its distortions and deceptions, the digital realm offers unprecedented access to genuine teachings, established lineage holders, and time-tested practices from every tradition on earth. Never before in human history have seekers had such immediate access to the wisdom of masters, the guidance of legitimate teachers, and the company of serious practitioners from around the globe—from North America's evidence-based approaches to Europe's privacy-focused implementations to Asia-Pacific's integration of traditional medicine with family-oriented wellness.

The question isn't whether to engage with this technology, but how to do so without losing our souls in the process. The answer, as with most spiritual endeavors, lies not in the tools themselves but in the structure we build around their use. Just as physical fitness requires consistent practice within a carefully designed framework—not random bursts of intense activity followed by weeks of neglect—spiritual development demands the same disciplined architecture.

Consider how physical transformation actually occurs: through daily commitment to specific exercises, performed with proper form, progressing gradually from simple to complex movements, always respecting the body's current capacity while gently pushing its edges. The person who attempts advanced Olympic lifts without building foundational strength inevitably injures themselves. The person who works out intensely for a week then abandons practice for months never develops real fitness. Progress comes from showing up consistently to unglamorous, repetitive practices that slowly, imperceptibly build capacity over time.

Spiritual development follows identical principles. The most profound teachings in the world, whether encountered through a screen or in person, remain useless without the daily, unglamorous work of actual practice. The seeker who consumes advanced tantric concepts without years of basic meditation training, who attempts plant medicine ceremonies without cultivating sobriety and emotional stability, who proclaims themselves a teacher after weekend workshops—they inevitably injure themselves and others, just like the amateur attempting professional athletic feats.

International research confirms this approach. Meta-analytic evidence from 14 studies involving 5,355 participants reveals a significant negative correlation between mindfulness and problematic social media use, though substantial cross-cultural variation indicates that cultural factors significantly influence intervention effectiveness. Chinese research with 446 college students identified specific pathways: mindfulness reduces social media addiction through improved attention control, reduced FOMO, and combined effects—patterns confirmed across Lebanese, Ethiopian, and Australian studies.

The key lies in using digital spiritual resources to support a committed daily practice rather than substituting for one—returning always to the silence that no algorithm can penetrate, where our own inner wisdom waits with infinite patience to be discovered.

The soul, it turns out, cannot be swiped into awakening. Enlightenment resists downloading, hash-tagging, or viral sharing. But when we approach digital spiritual resources with the same discipline we'd bring to physical training—with structure, consistency, humility, and respect for proper progression—these platforms can serve genuine transformation rather than spiritual fantasy.

The deepest truths emerge not from consuming endless spiritual content but from using that content to support committed practice. The silence between posts, the space between scrolls, the unglamorous daily return to our own breathing—this is where the real work happens, beyond the reach of any algorithm, in the depths of our own being where transformation has always been waiting.

What Can't Be Sold

After wandering through the digital midway where everyone performs their seeking for an audience of other performers, you might find yourself standing in an unexpected place: nowhere. The notifications have been silenced, the endless scroll has stopped, and suddenly you're alone with nothing but the echoing silence of your own confusion. Without the constant stream of spiritual content to consume, without the next teacher to follow or technique to try, you're faced with the most radical question of all — who are you when no one is watching and there's nothing left to collect?

This is where the real spiritual path begins. Not in the curated feed of mystical insights, not in the next workshop promising transformation, not even in the perfectly positioned crystals catching morning light. It begins in the unglamorous, un-postable moment when you stop regurgitating other people's wisdom and start confronting your own patterns, habits, and unconscious choices that have been running your life while you were busy seeking enlightenment elsewhere.

The carnival taught us what to look out for — the fortune tellers, the weekend warriors, the compound gurus, and the algorithmic attention merchants. It showed us how spiritual entertainment masquerades as the real path, how collecting experiences can become a substitute for actual transformation. Now, for those ready to move beyond the distractions, we must build something sturdy on the cleared ground, something that can weather the storms of ordinary life and the subtle earthquakes of actual growth.

What follows isn't another spiritual system to collect or technique to master. It's a return to the basics that every wisdom tradition has always pointed toward, though each wrapped them in their own cultural language and practices. What we're doing here is stripping away that cultural packaging to present these principles as simply as possible: the fundamental architecture of human development that makes everything else possible.

Think of it as learning to walk before attempting to dance, or tuning your instrument before joining the orchestra. These aren't preliminary exercises you graduate from—they're the foundation that supports whatever genuine practice calls to you, whether that's meditation, prayer, service, art, or simply living with greater awareness and compassion.

The path we're reclaiming is both ancient and immediate, both universal and deeply personal. It requires nothing you don't already possess and everything you've been avoiding. It asks not for your devotion to another teacher's vision, but for your commitment to becoming the author of your own story.

Taking Responsibility

The spiritual path begins with the most ordinary and extraordinary act possible: admitting that you are responsible for the quality of your own experience. Not responsible for everything that happens to you—earthquakes, economic crashes, and other people's choices lie beyond your control. But responsible for how you meet what comes, what you do with what you've been given, and the energy you bring to each moment of your life.

This isn't the self-punishing responsibility that blames you for every misfortune or demands perfection. It's the empowering recognition that you are the driver of your own life, not a passenger hoping someone else knows the way. Personal responsibility is like being the designated driver for your own existence—it's less fun at first, but at least you wake up knowing how you got home.

Most of us have spent years practicing elaborate forms of avoidance, perfecting the art of being everywhere except where we actually are. We doom-scroll until our thumbs ache, convincing ourselves we're staying informed when we're really hiding from the discomfort of our own unresolved feelings. We analyze ourselves endlessly instead of changing anything. We wait for the right mood, the right moment, the right teacher, the right practice— anything except taking the next obvious step with what we already know.

The first sign of spiritual maturity is realizing that no one is coming to save you from yourself. No guru, no practice, no insight, no achievement will do the work of actually inhabiting your own life. Like an editor who can't fix a blank page, no teacher can guide a student who refuses to show up for their own experience.

But here's where responsibility becomes revolutionary rather than burdensome: it transforms you from victim to author. Instead of hoping your circumstances will change so you can finally be happy, you begin changing how you meet your circumstances. Instead of waiting for others to create the conditions for your peace, you start creating those conditions yourself, one small choice at a time.

The ripple effects of this shift extend far beyond personal comfort. When you stop leaking your unprocessed emotions onto everyone around you, your relationships improve. When you take ownership of your energy instead of expecting others to manage your moods, you become someone people actually want to be around. When you handle your responsibilities without resentment or martyrdom, you free up mental space for creativity, compassion, and the kind of presence that makes ordinary moments feel sacred.

This begins with micro-responsibilities—small promises to yourself that you actually keep. Saying you'll make your bed and making it. Committing to a five-minute walk and taking it. Deciding to put your phone away during meals and following through. These tiny acts of self-integrity build trust in your own word, creating the foundation for larger commitments to emerge naturally.

The practice isn't about becoming perfect; it's about becoming honest about where you are and what you're actually willing to do about it. Responsibility means acknowledging that every choice creates consequences, that every habit shapes character, and that every moment offers the opportunity to respond rather than react to life's inevitable challenges.

Avoiding responsibility is like trying to parallel park while blindfolded—you might eventually squeeze in somewhere, but you'll definitely hit something along the way. Taking responsibility is like finally admitting you've been driving with the parking brake on—it explains why everything felt so much harder than it needed to be.

When you fully embrace authorship of your own story, something shifts at the cellular level. You stop waiting for permission to live fully. You stop expecting others to guess what you need. You stop hoping that external achievements will solve internal confusion. Instead, you begin the patient, unglamorous, profoundly liberating work of becoming the person you were always capable of being—starting exactly where you are, with exactly what you have, right now.

Living in Integrity

True spirituality begins not in meditation halls or sacred ceremonies, but in the unglamorous moments of daily life—how you treat the cashier when you're running late, what you do when no one will know you cut corners, whether your private thoughts align with your public persona. Integrity isn't about moral superiority or perfect behavior; it's about structural soundness, the alignment between your inner values and outer actions that creates a stable foundation for everything else.

Living without integrity is like looking in a funhouse mirror—you recognize yourself, but everything appears distorted, making it impossible to see clearly what needs attention or adjustment. When your actions contradict your stated values, when your words don't match your behavior, when you present one version of yourself to the world while harboring another internally, you create a kind of spiritual static that drowns out any chance of clarity or peace.

Consider how much mental energy gets consumed when you're living in contradiction with yourself. Part of your consciousness has to constantly monitor and manage the gap between who you say you are and who you actually are. This internal surveillance system runs in the background like a computer virus, slowing down everything else—your decision-making becomes muddier, your relationships feel more effortful, your sense of direction gets cloudier.

Integrity provides the stable center that keeps you grounded when life gets chaotic. Without it, you become like a person trying on different personalities at a party—you might look interesting as you sample every conversation and adopt every opinion you encounter, but you never develop the depth that comes from knowing who you actually are. When real challenges arise, you have no solid sense of self to draw from, just a collection of borrowed ideas and temporary identities that dissolve under pressure.

The practice of integrity begins with micro-alignments—small promises to yourself that you actually keep. If you say you're going to exercise, exercise. If you commit to calling your mother, call her. If you decide to eat mindfully, put the phone away during meals. These aren't trivial commitments; they're trust-building exercises between you and yourself. Each kept promise strengthens your confidence in your own word, while each broken promise erodes it.

This erosion goes deeper than simple disappointment. When you consistently fail to honor your own commitments, you develop a corrosive lack of self-respect that seeps into every area of life. You stop believing you're capable of change, stop trusting your own judgment, stop taking your own goals seriously. This internal collapse of confidence shows up as procrastination, self-sabotage, and a persistent sense that you're not the kind of person who follows through on important things.

Worse, this lack of internal integrity inevitably destroys trust in your relationships with others. People sense when someone doesn't keep faith with themselves—if you can't be trusted to honor your own word, why would anyone believe you'll honor your word to them? The person who constantly breaks small promises to themselves becomes unreliable in partnerships, friendships, and professional relationships, creating a cycle where external rejection reinforces internal self-doubt.

But integrity goes deeper than keeping commitments. It's about showing up honestly rather than performing the version of yourself you think others want to see. It means speaking truthfully even when lies would be more convenient, choosing kindness even when cruelty would feel more satisfying, admitting mistakes even when you could probably get away with hiding them.

This honesty creates a strange efficiency in life. When you're not maintaining multiple versions of yourself, when you don't have to remember what story you told to whom, when your values provide consistent criteria for decision-making, everything becomes simpler. You stop second-guessing yourself constantly because you're operating from a coherent center rather than a collection of conflicting impulses.

The spiritual marketplace often confuses integrity with rigid adherence to rules, turning it into another form of spiritual materialism where you collect moral achievements like merit badges. But true integrity is responsive, not robotic. It's about knowing your core principles well enough to bend without breaking, to adapt to circumstances while maintaining your essential character.

Sometimes integrity means disappointing people who expect you to maintain comfortable lies. Sometimes it means admitting you don't know something when pretending knowledge would be easier. Sometimes it means choosing the harder path because it aligns with who you're committed to becoming, not who you've been.

The temple of lasting spiritual development can only be built on the bedrock of integrity. Without this foundation, every practice becomes performance, every insight becomes entertainment, every moment of growth collapses back into the same old patterns. But when your foundation is solid—when your actions consistently reflect your deepest values—you can weather any criticism, any setback, any temptation without losing your center.

Integrity isn't about becoming perfect; it's about becoming whole. It's the difference between a cracked foundation that looks fine until pressure is applied, and solid ground that can support whatever you choose to build upon it. When you live with integrity, you stop leaking energy through the cracks of self-contradiction and start channeling that power toward whatever matters most to you.

This is where the spiritual path stops being about collecting experiences and starts being about becoming the kind of person who can handle whatever experiences arise with grace, honesty, and an unshakeable sense of who you are beneath all the changing circumstances of life.

Cultivating Inner Discipline

Spiritual work isn't about comfort—it's about discipline forged through consistent effort, turning the chaos of scattered impulses into the order of intentional living. But discipline in the spiritual context has been misunderstood, twisted into images of rigid self-punishment and joyless restriction or suppression. True discipline isn't about becoming a drill sergeant to yourself; it's about devotion showing up in ordinary, repeatable acts that slowly shape your inner landscape.

Building discipline is like watering a plant—consistent care creates strength and resilience, while neglect leads to gradual withering. You might not notice the effects of skipping a day or two, but over time the cumulative impact becomes undeniable. The plant that receives regular attention develops deep roots and can weather storms that would topple something left to chance. Small acts of self-care compound into resilience. Small choices toward order compound into clarity. Small moments of restraint compound into freedom from compulsion.

Consider the difference between discipline and rigidity. Discipline is responsive, like water finding its way around obstacles while maintaining its essential direction toward the sea. Rigidity is brittle, like ice that looks strong but shatters under pressure. True discipline bends without breaking, adapts to circumstances while holding to core principles, knows when to push forward and when to rest.

The practices that build inner discipline are deceptively simple: cleanliness of body and space, conscious moderation in desires and consumption, gratitude for daily blessings, quiet self-reflection at day's end. These aren't exotic techniques requiring special training —they're human basics that create the foundation for everything else. Without them, advanced spiritual pursuits become like trying to tune a guitar with broken strings; no amount of virtuosity will make the music sing.

What you feed yourself becomes what you are. This includes not just food, but thoughts, media, conversations, environments. Expecting inner peace while consuming negativity is like planting flowers in soil you've poisoned, then wondering why nothing beautiful grows. Nourishing inputs create resilience and clarity. Toxic inputs erode focus and vitality, making genuine spiritual development nearly impossible.

Digital discipline deserves special attention in our current era. The endless scroll trains restless seeking, constant stimulation, perpetual dissatisfaction with the present moment. Creating boundaries around technology use isn't about becoming a digital hermit—it's about preserving the mental space necessary for reflection, contemplation, and the kind of sustained attention that allows wisdom to emerge.

Environmental discipline matters more than most realize. The state of your living space reflects and shapes the state of your inner world—the relationship flows both directions. Clutter creates mental static. Cleanliness creates clarity. Sometimes organizing your outer world is easier than organizing your inner world because it's more straightforward and linear. You can see immediate results from cleaning a room, filing papers, or creating order in your physical space. This outer work then begins to influence your inner landscape, creating structure and calm bit by bit.

A clean environment is like setting the stage for a performance or starting a painting with a clean canvas. When the stage is properly set and the canvas is prepared, that's when your best potential can shine. This isn't about perfectionism or obsessive organization—it's about creating the conditions where clarity and focus can naturally emerge. A person who can't maintain basic order in their physical environment will struggle to cultivate order in their mental and emotional landscape, but the reverse is equally true: bringing order to your outer world can be the catalyst for bringing peace to your inner world.

The discipline of restraint teaches discrimination—the ability to distinguish between genuine needs and manufactured wants, between nourishing desires and destructive cravings. This isn't about denying all pleasure or living in deprivation. It's about developing the capacity to choose consciously rather than being driven unconsciously by every impulse that arises.

But how does one determine which desires deserve attention and which should be set aside? This requires the conscious work of identifying your core values and principles and examining the root of each desire—what matters most to you when everything else is stripped away. Without a clear hierarchy of priorities, every impulse feels equally urgent, every craving seems justified, every want masquerades as a need.

This clarification process demands honest self-examination. What kind of person do you want to become? What experiences truly nourish your growth versus those that provide temporary pleasure but leave you emptier than before? What activities align with your deepest values versus those that conflict with who you're trying to be? These questions can't be answered abstractly—they require ongoing attention to how different choices actually affect your energy, relationships, and sense of purpose over time.

Once you've established this internal compass, restraint becomes less about rigid rule-following and more about intelligent navigation. You can distinguish between the legitimate need for rest versus the compulsive urge to escape responsibility, between healthy social connection versus addictive social media scrolling, between nourishing your body versus numbing uncomfortable emotions with food or substances.

Gratitude practice deserves recognition as one of the most powerful disciplinary tools available. The mind's default tendency is to focus on what's missing, what's wrong, what needs to be different. Regular gratitude practice interrupts this negativity bias, consciously redirecting attention toward abundance rather than scarcity, toward appreciation rather than complaint. This isn't about replacing one unconscious pattern with another—it's about bringing conscious awareness to where you place your attention. What begins as deliberate practice gradually transforms into a natural way of seeing, but the key is maintaining the conscious choice rather than letting it become another automatic response. This shift in awareness creates the psychological foundation for contentment, regardless of external circumstances.

Self-reflection at day's end creates the feedback loop necessary for genuine growth. Without honest assessment of how you spent your time and energy, patterns remain unconscious and change becomes impossible. This isn't about self-judgment or detailed journaling—it's about cultivating the practice of conscious review that allows learning from experience rather than merely accumulating it. The key is bringing deliberate awareness to this process rather than letting it become mechanical. Each evening's reflection is a fresh opportunity to observe your choices, notice patterns, and consciously adjust your direction, maintaining the element of choice and awareness that keeps the practice alive rather than automatic.

The compound effect of consistent discipline creates momentum that makes larger changes feel natural rather than forced. Each small victory builds confidence in your capacity for self-direction. Each kept commitment strengthens trust in your own word. Each moment of conscious choice expands your sense of agency in shaping your own experience.

But perhaps the most important aspect of inner discipline is understanding that it's not about perfection—it's about direction. The person who gets back on track after stumbling demonstrates more discipline than the person who never faces real temptation. Progress isn't measured by flawless execution but by persistent return to intention after inevitable lapses.

This disciplined foundation creates the inner stability necessary for deeper spiritual exploration. When you can manage your basic human functions with consistency and care—when you show up reliably for your own life—you develop the capacity to handle whatever insights, challenges, or opportunities emerge on the path ahead.

True discipline liberates rather than restricts. It frees you from being tossed around by every mood, every impulse, every external circumstance. It creates the solid ground from which conscious choice becomes possible, where freedom means the power to respond deliberately rather than react unconsciously to whatever life presents.

The Body as an Instrument

The body isn't the goal of spiritual development, but it is the vehicle for all experience. Neglecting it hinders the journey, while honoring it enhances clarity. This isn't about worship or vanity—it's about recognizing the body as your partner in consciousness rather than either your prison or your temple.

Treating your body like a rental car might work for a weekend, but it's a terrible long-term strategy. The person who fills themselves with processed food, avoids movement, and ignores signals of fatigue or stress creates a kind of static that drowns out subtler perceptions. It's like trying to tune into delicate frequencies with a broken radio—the interference overwhelms any chance of clear reception.

The difference between living in your body and carrying it around like luggage becomes apparent in moments of stress, challenge, or deep attention. When you're embodied, you feel integrated, responsive, present. When you're merely carrying your body around, you feel disconnected, reactive, somewhere else even when you're physically present.

This integration begins with basic respect for your body's signals and needs. Sleep when tired, eat when hungry, move when restless, rest when depleted. This sounds obvious, but most people have lost touch with these natural rhythms, substituting external schedules and social expectations for internal wisdom.

The goal isn't peak physical performance or aesthetic perfection—it's creating the conditions where your body supports rather than distracts from whatever you're trying to accomplish. A body poisoned by neglect or excess can't provide the stability and clarity needed for deeper exploration of consciousness. The fatigue, discomfort, and mental fog that result from poor physical care create constant interference with attention and awareness.

Strength, stillness, and balance in the body translate directly to steadiness in the mind. This isn't just some spiritual concept—it's observable fact. Try holding a challenging physical position with grace and notice what happens to your mental state. Try maintaining calm breathing under stress and observe how it affects your emotional reactivity. The body-mind connection isn't a spiritual concept; it's a practical reality that can be verified through direct experience.

But the body also teaches discrimination between different types of discomfort. There's the productive discomfort of growth—muscles adapting to new demands, flexibility increasing through gentle stretching, endurance building through appropriate challenge. Then there's the destructive discomfort of injury, exhaustion, or pushing beyond capacity. Learning to distinguish between these signals is essential both for physical health and spiritual development.

Many spiritual seekers swing between extremes—either ignoring the body entirely in pursuit of transcendent experiences, or becoming obsessed with physical optimization as another form of spiritual materialism. The middle way recognizes the body as an instrument that requires care and attention without becoming the sole focus of that attention.

Regular physical care transforms the body from obstacle to ally. Simple movements like walking in nature provide both exercise and contemplative awareness. Conscious breathing exercises offer both physical and mental benefits. Mindful eating becomes both nourishment and practice. The body becomes a teacher rather than a burden, offering constant feedback about the effects of your choices and the state of your overall system.

This feedback system only functions when you develop sensitivity to the subtle life that you are. The body continuously sends signals—shifts in energy, changes in breathing, variations in tension, fluctuations in alertness—but these messages are easily drowned out by excessive stimulation. Reducing stimulants like caffeine, digital overwhelm, and constant noise allows the nervous system to calm enough for you to perceive the more delicate communications your body is always transmitting. When you become sensitive to this subtle intelligence, you gain access to wisdom that goes far beyond intellectual understanding.

The breath deserves special attention as the most immediate bridge between voluntary and involuntary processes, between conscious and unconscious functioning. How you breathe directly affects your nervous system, your mental state, your emotional reactivity, and your capacity for sustained attention. Yet most people breathe in ways that create tension, anxiety, and scattered focus without realizing the connection.

Posture, too, influences consciousness more than most recognize. The way you hold yourself affects not just physical comfort but mental clarity and emotional balance. Slumped posture creates mental sluggishness. Rigid posture creates mental tension. Balanced, relaxed uprightness supports both alertness and ease—the optimal state for most activities requiring sustained attention.

The ancient insight that the body houses consciousness takes on practical meaning when you begin treating your physical form as the sanctuary it is. Not through ritualistic worship or excessive concern, but through the kind of respectful maintenance you'd give to any valuable instrument. Keep it clean, provide proper fuel, allow adequate rest, give it appropriate challenges, and listen to its feedback.

This approach naturally leads to what might be called body wisdom—the ability to sense what nourishes versus what depletes, what strengthens versus what weakens, what supports clarity versus what creates confusion. Your body becomes a sophisticated guidance system, offering information about choices, environments, relationships, and activities that goes far beyond intellectual analysis.

When the body is cared for consciously but not obsessively, it becomes transparent to deeper experiences. Like a clean window that allows clear vision or a tuned instrument that produces pure sound, a well-maintained body gets out of the way of whatever you're attempting to perceive, understand, or express.

This is the practical meaning of treating the body as instrument rather than goal. The violin isn't separate from the music it creates—together they form one seamless expression. The body is consciousness taking physical form, not separate from awareness but awareness expressing itself in matter. Every cell processes information, every organ coordinates intelligently, every breath connects invisible life force with visible form—all expressions of the same underlying intelligence appearing at different levels of density. Care for this embodied awareness not as a vessel to be optimized for spiritual goals, but as consciousness itself learning to know itself through form.

Breath as the Bridge

Breath is the most immediate link between body, mind, and the subtle energies that animate your existence—it's always present, yet often overlooked as a tool for transformation. While you can survive weeks without food and days without water, you can't survive minutes without breath. Yet most people breathe in ways that create tension, scatter attention, and amplify emotional reactivity without ever making the connection.

Ignoring your breath while trying to find inner peace is like looking for your glasses while they're on your head—the tool you need is already there, functioning automatically, waiting for conscious engagement. Every moment offers the opportunity to use breath as an anchor, a reset button, a bridge between reactive patterns and conscious response.

Pay attention to how you breathe when you're stressed versus when you're calm. Anxiety comes with quick, shallow breaths that barely reach your chest. Anger makes breathing tight and irregular. Scattered thinking pairs with scattered breathing. But when you're truly relaxed and focused, breathing becomes deeper and steadier without you even trying. This connection works both ways—your mental state affects your breathing, but your breathing also affects your mental state. Change one, and you change the other. This illustrates the psychosomatic and somatopsychic loops we constantly navigate. Psychosomatic refers to how our mental state affects our body—stress creating shallow breathing, for instance. Somatopsychic is the reverse: how our body affects our mind— deeper breathing naturally calming our thoughts.

The breath operates at the intersection of voluntary and involuntary processes. You can control it consciously, yet it continues automatically when your attention is elsewhere. This unique position makes breath the perfect bridge between conscious and unconscious functioning, between the mind and the body, between surface experience and deeper states of awareness.

Ever notice how, when anxious, your breathing pattern resembles a squirrel on caffeine—quick, shallow, irregular? This breathlessness literally starves your system of the oxygen needed for clear thinking while signaling your nervous system to maintain high alert. Simply bringing conscious attention to breath and gradually deepening it can shift your entire physiological state within minutes.

Breath awareness during routine activities transforms ordinary moments into opportunities for presence and centered awareness. Breathing consciously while washing dishes, walking, waiting in line, or sitting in traffic creates islands of calm in the midst of daily demands. These micro-practices accumulate over time, building the capacity to remain centered even during challenging circumstances.

The ancient understanding of breath as life-force rather than mere air exchange reveals something most modern people have forgotten. Traditional practices across cultures recognized breath as the key to unlocking deeper states of concentration, calming the mind for meditation, and accessing the subtle energies that sustain life itself. How you breathe shapes not just your physical health but your mental clarity, emotional stability, and capacity for sustained attention. Masters of various traditions used specific breathing techniques to prepare for deep states of stillness, to cultivate inner energy, and to maintain unwavering focus during extended practice. The person who learns to work skillfully with breath gains access to immediate shifts in awareness and physiological state without depending on external circumstances to provide calm or clarity.

Breath serves as an anchor during emotional storms, providing a stable point of focus when thoughts and feelings become turbulent. Rather than being swept away by internal weather patterns, you can return attention to the steady rhythm of inhalation and exhalation, using breath as both refuge and reset mechanism. This isn't about suppressing emotions but about maintaining conscious awareness while they move through your system.

The quality of your breath directly affects the quality of your presence. Rushed, shallow breathing creates rushed, shallow engagement with whatever you're doing. Calm, deep breathing supports calm, deep engagement. This makes breath regulation one of the most practical tools for improving performance, relationships, and decision-making across all areas of life.

Simple breath techniques can be practiced anywhere without special equipment or training. Equal-length inhalation and exhalation creates balance and stability. Slightly longer exhalation than inhalation activates the parasympathetic nervous system, promoting relaxation and recovery. Conscious breathing during transitions between activities helps maintain awareness rather than moving unconsciously from one thing to the next.

But perhaps most importantly, breath awareness may serve as an accessible bridge between conscious and unconscious processes. Research shows that controlled breathing techniques can influence both the autonomic nervous system—which manages unconscious functions like heart rate and blood pressure—and brain activity in areas that regulate internal bodily states. The mechanism appears straightforward: deep breathing stretches lung tissue, producing signals that synchronize neural elements and shift the nervous system toward a calmer, more balanced state. As you develop sensitivity to the relationship between breath patterns and your internal condition, you may access measurable information about stress and emotional regulation that conventional self-analysis misses—what contemplative traditions have long described as making the invisible visible.

The breath doesn't judge, doesn't require perfection, doesn't demand specific beliefs or practices. It simply offers itself as a constant companion and teacher, available every moment for those willing to pay attention. In a world of endless distractions and complex spiritual techniques, the breath remains the most accessible, immediate, and reliable tool for returning to presence, clarity, and conscious awareness.

When you learn to use breath consciously, you discover that you carry within yourself the capacity to shift your state, regulate your nervous system, and access deeper levels of awareness regardless of external circumstances. This self-reliance isn't about isolation—it's about developing the inner stability that allows you to engage more fully with whatever life presents, from a place of centered awareness rather than reactive confusion.

The Path Reclaimed

This book has not been about giving you a pre-fabricated spiritual house or handing you some mystical blueprint with confusing instructions and missing pieces. Its aim has been to walk with you past the busy carnival streets filled with performers and onto the open land—so you can build something durable, sturdy, and livable within yourself. A space that shelters, strengthens, and grows with you rather than collapsing under the first real pressure.

You now know what to look for in the carnival. You've seen how the fortune tellers exploit uncertainty, how weekend warriors package transformation into consumable experiences, how compound gurus build empires from devotion, how psychedelic experiences can offer profound glimpses but can never do the fundamental work for you, and how digital platforms turn seeking itself into entertainment. You've learned to recognize the difference between spiritual substance and spiritual theater, between teachers pointing toward truth and performers selling fantasies.

But recognition isn't enough. Awareness without action remains academic. The real test comes when you step away from analyzing the carnival and begin building your own foundation. This is where most seekers hesitate—it's easier to attend another workshop than to face the raw responsibility of building your own inner structure that can endure life's inevitable storms.

There is a Sanskrit aphorism from the ancient Vedic tradition: *"Mana eva manushyanam karanam bandha mokshayoh"*—as the mind, so the person. Both bondage and liberation exist only in the mind. Not in your circumstances, your teacher, or your experiences. Your mind—the quality of attention you bring to each moment, the patterns you feed through daily choices. Others may influence your life, but your inner experience remains entirely your domain, and we can never expect outside intervention to free us from ourselves.

This truth echoes through every layer of existence, from the cosmic to the cellular. When an egg is cracked from outside forces—by circumstance, by someone else's agenda—life ends. But when that same egg cracks from within, life blossoms into its fullest potential. Look closely and you'll see this pattern everywhere: the seed that splits open from its own inner growth, not external pressure. The butterfly that must struggle free from its chrysalis through its own effort—any help from outside weakens the wings it needs to fly. The flower bud that opens when internal readiness meets the light, not when forced apart by impatient hands.

As above, so below. The same intelligence that governs the spiral of galaxies shapes the unfurling of ferns. The laws that move planets through their orbits move consciousness through its own expansion. We all live within shells of our own making—shells of assumption, limitation, familiar suffering—but the force that cracks them open must come from within. External spiritual interventions can only crack the shell from outside, leaving us broken rather than liberated. True transformation must emerge from your own awareness outgrowing unconscious patterns, your commitment to consciousness becoming stronger than attachment to what no longer serves.

The foundational elements—responsibility, integrity, discipline, body awareness, breath consciousness—aren't preliminary exercises you graduate from. They're ongoing infrastructure supporting whatever authentic practice calls to you, whether contemplative silence, creative expression, service to others, or simply living with greater awareness in ordinary circumstances.

This isn't about achieving some final enlightened state. Those experiences may come or they may not, but making them the goal turns the spiritual path into another ego quest. It's about developing capacity to remain awake to your own experience rather than sleepwalking through life on autopilot. It's about becoming the author of your own story rather than a character in someone else's spiritual drama.

Beyond the Circus

The path forward requires different courage than what the carnival promises. Not the dramatic courage of peak experiences, but the quiet courage of showing up for ordinary life every single day. The courage to face patterns without judgment, to change what needs changing without drama, to accept what can't be changed without resentment. The courage to be ordinary in a world that profits from making you feel special.

Your discernment has been sharpened through exposure to the carnival's illusions. Trust it completely. When something feels too easy or promises results disconnected from actual work required, when teachers focus more on their image than teaching, when practices promise escape rather than engagement—you recognize these red flags as invitations to turn inward.

But discernment works both ways. You can now recognize trustworthy guidance: the teacher who points beyond themselves toward your own capacity, the practice that increases your ability to handle ordinary challenges, the community that supports individual development rather than demanding conformity, the path that makes you more yourself rather than a copy of someone else.

The foundation you're building won't guarantee life becomes easy, but it ensures you become capable of handling whatever life presents. Challenges will still arise. Emotions will continue moving through your system. But you'll meet these experiences from centered awareness rather than reactive confusion, conscious choice rather than unconscious compulsion.

This is the great reclamation: taking back your spiritual development from those who would package and sell it back to you. Recognizing that wisdom isn't always hidden in exotic locations or ancient secrets—it's woven into the very fabric of existence, visible in every natural process that unfolds from within rather than being imposed from without. It's available in the quality of attention you bring to washing dishes and sweeping floors, the presence you offer in conversations, the consciousness you maintain while breathing. Wisdom is as immediate as your next breath—present, accessible, requiring no special techniques or teachers.

The journey that began with curiosity about spiritual possibilities culminates in recognizing you were never seeking anything outside yourself. Every earnest teacher was pointing toward your own capacity for awareness. Every practice was training your own attention. Every tradition was describing what you already possess but had forgotten how to access—the same force that opens flowers, that spirals galaxies, that transforms caterpillars into butterflies. The universe does not evolve through external pressure but through consciousness recognizing and expressing its own infinite potential.

The circus will continue its performances, the marketplace will keep hawking its wares, the digital midway will keep flashing its attractions. But you now move through these spaces with quiet confidence of someone who has somewhere else to go—not away from the world, but deeper into authentic engagement with it.

The temple you build won't be impressive to carnival-goers. It won't photograph well for social media. It won't generate followers or admiration. But it will be yours—solid, livable, and strong enough to shelter your awakening consciousness.

Your mind holds both the prison and the key. Others may influence circumstances, but the quality of your inner experience— bound or free, reactive or responsive, unconscious or awake— remains your domain entirely. The ancient wisdom knew this: liberation and bondage arise from the same source, and that source is always your own willingness to pay attention.

Leave the carnival grounds behind with their flashing lights and endless promises of transformation for sale. The open land awaits beyond the gates, quiet and spacious, where you can cultivate your own grounded temple of practice—not cracked open by external force, but blossoming from within through your own courageous commitment to conscious living. Here you join the vast community of all things that transform according to their own inner nature: the seed cracking its own hull to reach toward light, the snake shedding its skin when it outgrows its current form, consciousness awakening to its own infinite depth.

You don't need permission to begin living consciously. You don't need credentials to pay attention to your breath. You don't need initiation to take responsibility for your own experience. The path is open, full of infinite possibilities, and the only person who can walk it is you.

Notes

Market & Industry Data

• Global wellness economy: Reached $6.3 trillion in 2023, up from $4.4 trillion in 2020, with forecast to hit $9 trillion by 2028 (Global Wellness Institute, December 2024)

• Global spiritual services market: $376 billion in 2024, projected $787.4 billion by 2035 (Transparency Market Research, Global Growth Insights)

• Spiritual products and services market: $180.18 billion in 2024, expected to reach $249.03 billion by 2032 at 4.4% CAGR (Business Research Insights, Grand View Research)

• Spiritual wellness apps: Projected $4.84 billion by 2030 (14.4% CAGR) (Grand View Research)

• Global coaching practitioners: 122,974 certified globally, 15% increase since 2023 (International Coach Federation, 2025)

• Regional wellness spending per capita: North America $5,108, Europe $1,596, Asia-Pacific $399, Latin America $476 (Global Wellness Institute 2024)

Social Media & Digital Trends

• Spiritual hashtag views: #spirituality 48.4 billion views, #spiritual 19.1 billion views on TikTok (TikTok Hashtags analytics, 2024-2025)

• Wellness industry social media: TikTok 4.0% monthly growth, 18% nano-influencer engagement (Dash Social, Socialsnowball 2025)

• US Gen Z spiritual identification: 77% spiritual vs. 68% religious (Pew Research Center 2025, 36-nation study)

• Digital spiritual entrepreneurship: Virtual services 56.5% market share, 74% increase in audio/video practitioner usage (industry surveys)

Psychological & Neuroscience Research

• Attention span research: Debunks "8 seconds" claim (King's College London, Frontiers in Psychology meta-analyses)

• Brief meditation effectiveness: 13-minute daily meditation shows measurable benefits (Basso et al. 8-week study)

• Mindfulness and social media addiction: Meta-analysis of 14 studies (5,355 participants) shows correlation $r = -0.37$ (PMC systematic review)

• Spiritual bypassing concept: Term coined by psychologist John Welwood (1984) describing use of spiritual practices to avoid psychological work

Clinical Psychedelic Research

• Psilocybin depression treatment: 75% treatment response and 58% remission rates at 12 months for major depressive disorder (Johns Hopkins - Davis et al. 2021, Gukasyan et al. 2022)

• MDMA PTSD treatment: 71.2% of participants no longer met PTSD criteria vs. 47.6% placebo group (Mitchell et al. 2021, Nature Medicine)

• Default Mode Network: Brain imaging shows psychedelics significantly reduce DMN activity, correlating with ego-dissolution experiences (Mason et al. 2021, Neuropsychopharmacology reviews)

Cult Awareness & High-Control Groups

• Cult involvement statistics: 0.5% to 3% lifetime involvement estimated, 3,000 to 5,000 destructive groups in US (cult awareness literature, ICSA resources - specific peer-reviewed validation requires further verification)

• BITE Model: Steven Hassan's framework for evaluating authoritarian control through Behavior, Information, Thought, and Emotional manipulation (developed from brainwashing research)

• Dark Triad personality research: Narcissism, Machiavellianism, and psychopathy as overlapping but distinct manipulative traits (Paulhus & Williams 2002)

• 3HO organization investigation: Over 300 witness testimonies regarding founder Yogi Bhajan allegations (An Olive Branch 2020, anolivebranch.org)

• Kundalini syndrome documentation: Medical literature documents "Kundalini psychosis" symptoms including mood swings, confusion, anxiety, hallucinations (psychiatric and consciousness studies research)

Note: All statistics were current as of publication date. Given rapidly evolving digital platforms and spiritual services markets, specific numbers may have changed since research compilation. Fundamental trends and patterns remain consistent across multiple studies and time periods.

General Research Sources While this book prioritizes narrative flow over academic citation, readers interested in deeper exploration may find value in these research areas:

Digital Technology and Attention: Frontiers in Psychology - Digital technology effects meta-analyses Clinical Psychological Science - Media multitasking research Developmental Psychology - Cross-cultural attention studies

Mindfulness and Technology: Mindfulness journal - Brief meditation intervention studies Journal of Behavioral Addictions -

Social media and mindfulness research Clinical Psychology Review - Mindfulness intervention effectiveness

Global Spirituality and Religion: Pew Research Center - International religious and spiritual trends Ipsos Global Religion Surveys - Cross-cultural belief systems Journal for the Scientific Study of Religion - Contemporary spirituality research

Wellness and Spiritual Services Markets: Global Wellness Institute - International wellness market reports McKinsey & Company - Consumer wellness trend analysis Transparency Market Research - Spiritual services market forecasts

Social Media and Influencer Marketing: Journal of Interactive Marketing - Influencer effectiveness studies Platform-specific analytics reports (TikTok, Instagram, YouTube) Digital marketing industry benchmark studies

Cult Awareness and Recovery: International Cultic Studies Association - Cult research and recovery resources Freedom of Mind Resource Center - Undue influence and cult recovery Academic journals on new religious movements and high-control groups

Readers seeking specific study details or methodologies are encouraged to search academic databases using the research areas and journal names listed above, as well as consulting the original market research reports from the organizations mentioned.